THE BLOEDEL RESERVE

Gardens in the Forest

November 7, 1988

Prof. Sally Schauman
348 Gould Hall JO-34
University of Washington
Seattle, WA 98195

Dear Sally:

This book has been published by the Arbor Fund coincident with the open-ing of the Bloedel Reserve to the general public on October 15, 1988. In-tended for sale at the Reserve and in book stores, it tells how the house came to be built on the bluff at Agate Point and describes, with the help of photographs and drawings, what people will see when they enter the new gate and pass by the new Gate House.

In a large way, it was conceived as a tribute to what Virginia and Prentice have accomplished, but it also takes note of the contributions of others who, like yourselves, have participated in the creation of the gardens.

Yours sincerely,

Bagley Wright

THE BLOEDEL RESERVE

Gardens in the Forest

by Lawrence Kreisman

Published by
The Arbor Fund
The Bloedel Reserve

Library of Congress Catalog in Publications Number
88-071534

Hard-bound ISBN 0-9621076-0-3
Soft-cover ISBN 0-9621076-1-1

Designed by Virginia Hand
Type set by Art-Foto Typography
Color Separations by Color Services
Printed by Heath Printers

ACKNOWLEDGEMENTS

As with the gardens of the Bloedel Reserve themselves, this publication has been a team endeavor, grown and nurtured by the invaluable contribution of many people. David Streatfield, Associate Professor of Landscape Architecture spent many hours walking the grounds of the Reserve. He reviewed countless conceptual schemes and drawings to establish a proper chronology of events and to document the planting materials that the visitor would see on walks through the Reserve. Richard Brown, Director of the Reserve, shared freely of his understanding of the Bloedels and their purpose, and of the many changes to the grounds during his tenure from 1976 to the present. Mary Randlett, who grew up near the Collins estate and has been photographing the Reserve and the Bloedel family since the 1960s, never faltered in her enthusiasm for this project nor in her efforts to capture the beauty and tranquility of the setting. *Architectural Digest* granted permission to publish some of the color photographs taken by Dick Busher for a 1984 article on the Reserve. Virginia Hand has designed a handsome background to the story and a subtle frame for the exquisite visual images. Casper Clarke shared many albums of Collins family photographs. Richard Brown, Mary Randlett, Virginia Clarke Younger, Mrs. Bayley Willis, Dennis Andersen, Dena Dawson, and Bagley and Virginia Wright read and made comments during the preparation of the manuscript.

TABLE OF CONTENTS

INTRODUCTION

Michelangelo envisioned his sculpted figures as hidden in the rough stone, simply waiting for the master stone carver's chisel to free them and reveal them to the world. A garden such as the one you enjoy at the Bloedel Reserve deserves to be seen in the same way. For in the rough-hewn setting of cedar, alder, and hemlock and in the groundcover of moss, ferns, and needles, a remarkable landscape of varied and exquisite character has emerged—a garden that never appears self-conscious or obtrusive, but seems to belong to the place. For centuries, it seems, the land held hidden these ponds, glens, and hedges, all waiting to be revealed by the subtle and not so subtle process of thinning out trees and shrubs, molding and reforming the knolls and ravines, and creating meandering pathways to allow you the pleasure of their discovery.

As with any great creative effort, these gardens grow and mature. Unlike those works of art that are painted or sculpted to completion, the art of shaping the landscape is subtler and more difficult to achieve. There is no final and unchangeable product. The gardens are in themselves a process, never finished, always needing nurturing, discipline and maintenance. The landscape and its components change daily and with each season, and it is a privilege to share in these changes. Dew, rain and snow, sun, clouds and wind all affect the physical form of the garden and the atmosphere you may sense when you walk through it on any given day.

Unlike the more traditional arboretum or botanical garden, the Bloedel Reserve does not purport to be an educational or research facility with specimen gardens or comprehensive collections of flowers or plants. Here species have been selected for their color, texture, and size as elements of harmonious visual compositions, under the artistic supervision of designers knowledgeable about European and Asian landscape traditions. The gardens and woodland at the Reserve are intended to provide a place apart from the hectic business, social and family worlds that fill our lives. The Reserve is a tranquil, spiritual place of retreat, open for meditation and rest—a place for the close and unrushed observation of the natural world. A series of outdoor living rooms reflecting these traditions stimulate the senses and move the viewer with its varied richness. In Mr. Bloedel's own words,

> Its primary purpose is the creation and maintenance of a place where people enjoy natural beauty as evidenced by plants. It will specialize in the wildflowers, shrubs, and trees native to this area and the woods, fields, and streams which are their natural environment … The Reserve as a whole should be an example of man working harmoniously with nature; where his power to manage is used cautiously and wisely … It would be our desire that through study, understanding and sympathetic treatment, the whole property would possess an internal unity and integrity that would realize its capacity to inspire and refresh.

Cyclamen

10

Aerial view of the residence and the bluff.

The manicured pathways and rustic trails of the Reserve lead you in a sequence that is as carefully contrived and controlled as the choreography of a ballet. The first major space you enter is a meadow — gentle and pastoral in spirit. It is a landscape that represents only the most gentle change from that outside the gates. The moss-covered woods beyond introduce you to the wilder qualities of a forest that was cut at an earlier period. You emerge from this woodland to the open Bird Marsh area — a part of the Reserve where the presence of a number of bird species takes dominance over the display of plants. Beyond the Bird Marsh, the south forest is wild and untamed, as nature reclaims and re-works the site of logging many years ago. Among these towering trees, you are reminded of the primeval forests of the Northwest, so few of which remain intact.

As the path leads out of the forest, you encounter lakes, gardens around the house, a bluff walk, Rhododendron Glen, Orchid Walk, the Japanese Garden, Moss Garden, and Reflection Pool — all contrived spaces seemingly carved out of the forest. Their presence and the order in which they are experienced provide a series of counterpoints to the experience of wild nature. There is the hushed serenity of the Orchid Walk and the abstract regularity of the Reflection Pool. The well-trimmed lawns and planned informality of gardens and ponds adjacent to the house partly reflect the English and French traditions inspired by the house style itself — nature adapted to create aesthetic effects. At the lake gardens and in the Rhododendron Glen, the addition of carefully placed ornamental plants establishes a different mood, one of accommodation with nature. Here, the manipulation of plant materials subtly establishes a balance between people and nature.

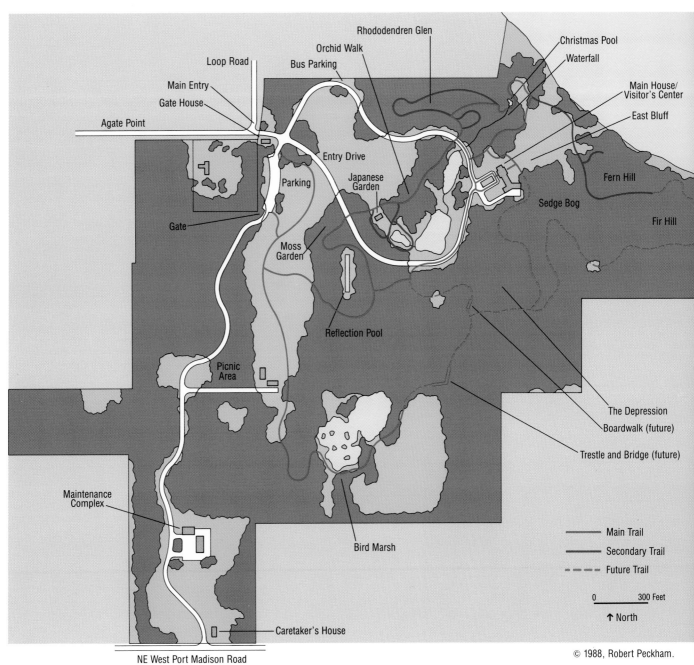

Rhododendren Glen

Christmas Pool

Orchid Walk

Waterfall

Loop Road

Bus Parking

Main House/
Visitor's Center

Main Entry

East Bluff

Gate House

Agate Point

Entry Drive

Fern Hill

Parking

Japanese
Garden

Sedge Bog

Gate

Fir Hill

Moss
Garden

Reflection Pool

The Depression

Boardwalk (future)

Trestle and Bridge (future)

Picnic
Area

Maintenance
Complex

Main Trail

Secondary Trail

Future Trail

Bird Marsh

0   300 Feet

↑ North

Caretaker's House

NE West Port Madison Road

© 1988, Robert Peckham.

While it is helpful to understand the concepts that were explored and the process by which specific areas of the Reserve have evolved, it is quite possible to walk through the forest and glens, sit in the quiet of the Japanese gardens, observe the swans in the ponds and listen to the sound of running water in the streams without a guide. That is one of the principal delights of this place. Depending on your pace and resting stops, your walk can be as short as an hour or as long as the place or your mood invites you to linger. And it will.

The elm tree displays bright autumn foliage.

Jonquils blanket the earth alongside the north drive bridge.

DICK BUSHER

MARY RANDLETT

MARY RANDLETT

14

Sun filters through the trees of the old growth forest.

Stately elms frame the residence.

This Reserve has been designed to offer a joyous experience, whether you are city- or country-bred, whether you are a landscape professional or simply someone who appreciates nature's collected works. But the property is rich in other ways as well. Its French country house, on a bluff overlooking Port Madison Bay near Agate Pass, was an improbable undertaking in this wild forest setting in 1931, when its neighboring houses were small log and frame summer cabins. Its builders, the Collins family, wielded significant influence in Seattle and King County as pillars of the business community and society. The architect of the house, J. Lister Holmes, was one of Seattle's premier designers; his architectural achievements from 1922 until his death in 1986 span the waning years of Beaux Arts design in America, the bridge of streamlined modernism, and the heyday of the International Style. His work of the 1920s and 1930s brought European ideas into common use in Seattle's prestige neighborhoods. The Collins house, his first major commission in the French style, realized his success in the residential field.

The family histories of the Collins and Bloedel families give insight into the way this property has been used. The intentions of its strong-willed owners—people with dreams, convictions, and, most important, persistence—led to the building of the house and changes to the landscape over the past sixty years under the expert guidance of several outstanding landscape architects. This book describes the process by which such a garden grows. What began as the Bloedels' personal exploration of and experimentation with plantings and conservation techniques has developed into award-winning public gardens in the forest.

CHAPTER 1

FROM LONGHOUSE TO HUNTING LODGE

... Each part of the soil is sacred in the estimation of my people. Every hillside, every valley, every plain and grove, has been hallowed by some sad or happy event ... and when the last Red Man shall have perished ... these shores will swarm with the invisible dead of my tribe ... and when your children's children think themselves alone in the field, the store, the shop, upon the highway, or in the silence of the pathless woods, they will not be alone ... At night when ... you will think them deserted, they will throng with the returning hosts that once filled and still love this beautiful land.

from *Chief Sealth's Farewell Speech, 1855*

The country now before us presented a most luxuriant landscape, and was probably not a little heightened in beauty by the weather that prevailed. The whole had the appearance of a continued forest extending as far as the eye could reach.

from Captain George Vancouver, *A Voyage of Discovery to the North Pacific Ocean and round the world.*

The Land

Before white settlement of Puget Sound, the Suquamish Indian tribes inhabited that part of present-day Bainbridge Island that includes the Bloedel Reserve property. The parcels of land that make up the Reserve are located between two historic points, Agate Point to the north and West Port Madison to the south. In 1827, John Work recorded in his *Hudson Bay Company Journal of Occurances:*

> We stopped at the Soquamis village situated on the bay of the same name It consists of 4 houses, we saw only 8 or ten men, but understand several of the inhabitants were off fishing. Our object in stopping here was to get the chief (Chief Sealth) to accompany

us as an interpreter, but he was not at home. The houses are built of boards covered with mats.

The village referred to was probably a temporary Indian summer camp located at the mouth of the stream running through the present Bloedel Reserve property and emptying onto what was described as a beautiful shallow sandy beach with groves of huge cedar trees along the edges of a dry marsh and estuary. This eventually became the location of the Collins family hunting lodge north of and below the Reserve property.

Anemone

In January 1855, the Point Elliott Treaty established certain designated portions of the island as the Port Madison Indian Reservation with the understanding that lands outside this property would be deeded to the U. S. government. In July and August 1856, these lands — including the Bloedel Reserve property — were surveyed by James Tilton, Surveyor General. Much of the Bloedel land was held for the benefit of the Territorial University. In 1862, a large tract — 2,675 acres — was purchased by George Meigs from Daniel Bagley, President of the Board of Commissioners for University Lands, for approximately $4,000. The revenue realized from this land sale was probably used to set up the course of instruction at the University. The timber harvested from these lands was cut into saw logs at the Meigs mill at Port Madison and, according to Daniel Bagley's Cash Book, the lumber was shipped to Seattle where it was used to erect the first building of the university. The southeast portion of the present Reserve, later known as Alder Beach, was part of that state land. Ironically, this land came under the temporary ownership of the University of Washington over 100 years later as a gift from the Bloedel family.

SPECIAL COLLECTIONS AND PRESERVATION DIVISION, UNIVERSITY OF WASHINGTON LIBRARIES

Fish drying racks were a common sight in the Suquamish village at Eagle Harbor on Bainbridge Island early in the twentiety century.

Logging first growth timber in Kitsap County near Suquamish

COURTESY SUQUAMISH TRIBAL PHOTOGRAPHIC ARCHIVES

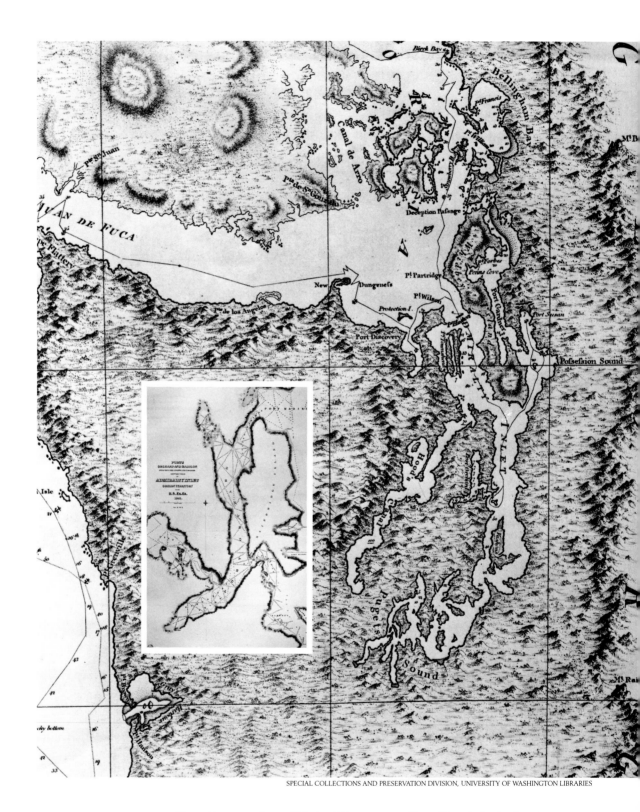

George Vancouver's chart, published in 1798, shows the area known as Bainbridge Island as a part of the Olympic Peninsula in 1792 before the discovery of the passage to the west.

Chart of Ports Orchard and Madison (inset), including the Inlets and Passages between them in Admiralty Inlet, Oregon Territory, 1841. From United States Exploring Expedition 1838-1842, *led by Charles Wilkes.*

Port Madison Mills, 1883. LaRoche photograph.

Meigs followed in the footsteps of his contemporary, Henry Yesler, whose first steam mill rose on Elliott Bay in 1853. That year, J. J. Felt established a steam-powered mill on Appletree Cove (now Kingston). Within a year, he found the moorage inadequate and the cove too shallow for loading lumber aboard sailing vessels. He sold out his interests to Meigs. The dismantled mill and equipment were barged seven miles south to Port Madison Bay. In his journal and in his *Narrative*, early Northwest explorer Captain Wilkes described Port Madison: "At this place a large and complete town arose, whose inhabitants depended wholly upon the activity of the mill for support, and who suffered and prospered as the mill itself met cataclysmic fires and booming trade." By

Engraving of the Pine Forest in Oregon (Territory) from the Charles Wilkes Narrative of the United States Exploring Expedition published in 1845.

Evening on Puget Sound, an Edward S. Curtis photograph c. 1899 in his Native American Indian Folio.

the 1850s, the local Indians had logged their shorelands, towing the cut timber by canoe to the Meigs mill. Some of them obtained work there as well. When Mrs. John Collins bought her property (now the Reserve lands) at the turn of the century, she described seeing the whole bay filled with sailing vessels waiting to discharge their ballast and take on lumber from the mill.

In addition to the land owned by George Meigs, a large number of tracts were purchased and resold over the next half-century on this part of Bainbridge, much of it eventually becoming part of the Bloedel Reserve. Eighty acres of the Agate Point Tracts that form the northern tip of the island were purchased in 1876 by Andrew Lunn and sold, in 1879, to William De Shaw, whose Bonanza

Trading Post at Agate Pass became a local landmark. In 1886, Shaw sold his holdings to a San Francisco speculator, E. R. Lilienthal. In 1905, Warren Gazzam, President of the Kitsap Transportation Company bought the Lilienthal holdings and platted Agate Point. Much of the present Reserve is located in the southernmost sector of this tract. It includes property originally purchased by William Ladd of Multnomah County in Oregon Territory and sold to logger Daniel Sackman, subsequently bought by Bailey Gatzert and the Schwabacher Brothers, Seattle's foremost merchants. Other early owners of Bloedel Reserve lands included William Inpett (1875), John Whoebeck (1877), H. Gabel (1872), and Julius Olson (1891). In 1890, William Bull purchased 160 acres, including the southeast portion of the Reserve. In 1892, Julius Olsen, William Bull, and the Gatzert-Schwabacher Land Co. gradually began to sell off their holdings in small 5-, 10-, and 20-acre parcels. Many Scandinavian names appeared on the records, and these lands primarily became small farms. In 1894, Charles Washington of Seattle became the first black man to own land in the Bainbridge community. His farm remained in family hands until 1975, when his heirs sold it to the Arbor Fund, the foundation that presently owns and manages the Reserve, to become part of the Reserve lands.

In 1905, William Trimble purchased a large parcel of land formerly owned by George Meigs from the London and San Francisco Bank, Ltd. Sold to V. Hugo Smith in the same year, some of this land was then platted as Alder Beach Tracts. Mrs. John Collins purchased from Trimble much of what is now Bloedel Reserve land. Some of the land was platted in 1914 in 2 1/2 acre tracts as Seabold Heights. After Mrs. Collins' death, the estate lands were purchased by Joshua Green and Bainbridge Island real estate agent Sam Clark, who sold the property in 1951 to Prentice and Virginia Bloedel.

T*he* Reliance *docking at Port Madison, ca. 1900.*

The Collins family in Seattle

In 1861, Angela Burdett-Coutts Jackling came to the Northwest with her parents. (Her namesake, Baroness Angela Burdett Coutts, was one of the greatest British philanthropists of the second half of the nineteenth century). Her uncle, Lawrence Grennan, had established sawmills at Utsaladdy on Camano Island — some claim they were the first on Puget Sound. In 1878, at the age of 18, she was married to 42-year old John Collins, a widower. By the time of their marriage, Collins was already a respected businessman and civic activist. An immigrant from Ireland, his American experience began by cutting timber and working in the sawmills in Machias, Maine. At the age of 22, he decided to try his luck in the timber rich wilderness of Puget Sound. The Machias firm of Pope and Talbot had established a mill and built a company town at Port Gamble. Arriving there, he found work for ten years with the Puget Sound Mill Company. His earnings were invested in a hotel there; he also had a major interest in the building of the Occidental Hotel in Seattle in 1865.

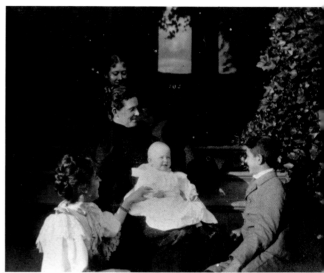

John Collins with sons John Francis (l.) and Bertrand (r.) at the side porch to the Minor Avenue house, 1896.

Angela Collins sits on the steps in front of the Minor Avenue residence, ca. 1892. Clockwise from top center: Edana, John Francis, Bertrand, and stepdaughter Emma.

His real estate holdings included the Seattle Hotel, rebuilt on the triangular site of the Occidental Hotel in 1889, the Collins Block on the site of his first home, and other valuable properties. He was one of the incorporators of the Seattle and Walla Walla Railroad, a move to counter the decision by the transcontinental railroad to place its terminus in Tacoma instead of Seattle. Although the line was never completed, its connection to Columbia City, Renton, and the coalfields at Newcastle stimulated the economy. Collins was involved with opening up and operating the Talbot and Cedar River coal mines and organized the first gas company. He also actively fought for a city-owned water supply, something that did not occur until after the disastrous 1889 fire. Collins was elected to the City Council for three successive terms. In 1877, he was elected the city's sixth mayor. He assisted in the drafting of a city charter and, as a representative to the Territorial Legislature during 1883-84, he urged a $6,000 appropriation for the University.

Mrs. Collins took her place in Seattle society beside her husband. Because of his friendship with President Cleveland, she spent much time in Washington D.C., and was called upon to act as hostess for notables who passed through Seattle. After her husband's death in 1903, she continued to entertain in high style in her famous blue drawing room on Minor Avenue, while raising four children — Edana, John Francis, Edward Bertrand (Bertie) and Catherine. From the recollections of her step-grandaughter, Virginia Clarke Younger, we have a fascinating picture of a strong, imposing, brilliant woman who asserted herself, a woman who expected her family and acquaintances to give her the respect and admiration she most assuredly had earned through her good works in the community.

By the time of her death in 1947, she had made a significant impact upon Seattle's social scene. But her greatest and most lasting contribution to the region was Collinswood, the country estate on Bainbridge Island that she dreamed about and which she, her son Bertrand, and architect J. Lister Holmes made a reality in a clearing overlooking the Sound.

A *lawn party at the Collins hunting lodge, ca. 1905.*

The Hunting Lodge at Agate Point

In 1904, Angela Collins bought 45 acres at Agate Point for a weekend and summer retreat on the beach. Later she purchased additional acreage adjoining it. According to Mrs. Younger's recollections, son John and stepdaughter Emma Downey expressed interest in the land as well. At Angela's suggestion then, the three of them drew straws for sections of the property. John and Emma both got beach property. Ironically, Mrs. Collins, who had bought the property originally because she wanted to be on the water, drew the property on the bluff with no access to the water.

John and a Scandinavian carpenter named Erickson proceeded to build a one-room beach house with a cedar shake roof and siding and a huge living/dining room with a fireplace at one end — for his frequent hunting and fishing expeditions. But it suited Mrs. Collins too, and according to her step-grandaughter, she simply "moved in."

At the time, there were few roads on the island and most transportation was by boat. There was a steamer that made a regular stop at the dock at Port Madison. Later on, there was also a stop at Agate Point. Groceries were ordered from Seattle and picked up at the Port Madison store on the *Clara Seagull*, the Collins family launch. Families living on Agate Point used an old Indian trail through the woods to the shore. At points it abutted the angular trail cut in the 1870s by the Puget Sound Telegraph and Cable Company when poles were strung for the cable system that would carry mill quotations to San Francisco lumber buyers and establish a telephone system on the island. The establishment of a ferry system by Kitsap County Transportation Company led to the cutting of a road from Port Blakely to Agate Point, and the first cars were brought over to the island.

The county road was hewn through swamp lands, cut-over timber lands, and second-growth forests. Many forested acres had been destroyed in a fire that originated in the burning of slashings during the clearing of the northern edge of 'The Collins Place' in the summer of 1910. The fire raced through the woods along the old Telegraph trail, jumping from tree to tree, burning straight down the center of Agate Point almost to the site of De Shaw's old trading store. The fire was stopped by volunteer fire-fighters—neighbors who came from nearby farms and summer camps. They controlled it by a back-fire set just above the Point. The present alder forest marks the course of that fire; fast-growing alders sprang up, smothering out the conifer seedlings. Fire burns are still visible on some of the stumps at the Bloedel Reserve. The present upper pond was the site of an alder bog that may have developed after the fire.

The old Indian trail ran from Agate Point to West Port Madison, directly opposite the site of the Meigs mill. It may have originated at William De Shaw's trading post or northeast of it, where the first steamer dock was located. This dock had been abandoned because the swift currents and exposure to strong north winds had made landing and tying up extremely difficult. A second dock was constructed several lots north of Mrs. Collins' property; the part of the trail between the old hunting lodge (later the site of Casper and Catherine Clarke's residence) and Agate Point dock was commonly used by the Collins and Clarke families. Residents in Port Madison recollected Indians from Suquamish canoeing to Agate Point, leaving their canoes on the beaches and walking along the trail to Port Madison to trade and buy at the only grocery store. During the years that the family used the beach house, Angela Collins described Port Madison Bay filled with black canoes of visiting Haida Indians. She recalled seeing the Indians building cedar canoes when she first bought the property. Members of the Collins family reportedly found many stone knives and chisels on the shore here. Catherine Clarke recalled her mother at one time talking with an old Indian woman who was paddling a canoe across the water in front of the lodge, headed for Port Madison.

> My mother was down on the beach and saw the woman going by and waved her in ... Because Mother did have a minimal vocabulary in the Indian language, she was able to talk to this aged woman, and the woman told her that the following winter was going to be terrible ... Mother asked her how she knew that ... She pointed up at the sky at some birds, some seagulls, and other birds that happened to be flying by. She seemed to be saying that the birds were a sign. Mother told me about it and more or less dismissed the idea that this aged Indian woman would be able to foretell the weather. However that winter (1916) was the worst winter that I ever recalled. The snow was so heavy that the dome of Saint James Cathedral in Seattle fell in.

CHAPTER 2

House in the Forest

Collinswood Takes Shape

Mrs. Collins and her son Bertie spent a good deal of time discussing construction of a permanent summer home on the property. After some disagreement as to its location, they decided that it should be built atop the bluff looking east across the Sound. The land on the bluff had been logged several times already, and no native growth forest stood in the way. But a stand of recent growth alder, then about 6-8 inches in diameter, had to be cleared to make way for the house.

Bertie Collins encouraged his mother to build a house in the French style and, although he had no architectural credentials, proposed to design it himself. Educated at Harvard with some coursework in design, Bertie had an eye for detail and a love of French Renaissance buildings that he acquired during his European travels. He planned a three-story house with formal entertaining in mind—a drawing room, a dining room, and a library on the ground floor, as well as butler's pantries and kitchen. The bedrooms were on the second floor, with a third floor that was intended to house the Clarke family. Knowing that he needed some technical assistance, Bertie observed recent construction in Seattle. A First Hill medical clinic in the French chateau style caught his attention. When he learned that the architect was J. Lister Holmes, he made an appointment to review some of his residential work. Impressed by it, Bertie presented Holmes to his mother and a pleasant relationship was established. The architect was contracted to transform Bertie's sketches into measured drawings and to oversee construction of the house.

J. Lister Holmes was a Seattle native who had been educated in Engineering at the University of Washington (1911) and received his architectural training at the University of Pennsylvania (1915). Here he had studied under the design head, Paul Crét, a Frenchman and an École des Beaux Arts graduate. Crét was one of the best known proponents of the Beaux Arts system in America. After seven years of practice in architectural offices in New York, Philadelphia, and Seattle, Holmes opened a private practice in 1922. By the late 1920s, he was already well known in Seattle circles for his excellent traditional residential work—most of it in the English or Norman style. The Collins house was his first major work in the French chateau idiom, and on the basis of its success, he was hired by the John Baillargeon family to do their new Washington Park home in that style. Then commissions followed in the Highlands, Broadmoor, Carlton Park Heights, Mount Baker, Mercer Island, and other exclusive neighborhoods. In 1954, when Holmes filled out the nominating application to become a Fellow of the American Institute of Architects, the first significant architectural achievement he listed was the Collins Residence of 1932. The nomination described his design achievements,

> By his understanding of proportions and planning relationships, the resultant work has the rare quality of fine beauty. Through such abilities varied designs have been successfully culminated—from earlier days of French styles to present day contemporary.

Common polypody

Charcoal rendering of Collinswood by artist Norman Fox, 1930.

Bertrand Collins at his typewriter, ca. 1930.

A Simple French Villa

The building that Bertie Collins desired and had Holmes build was a dignified, handsome residence in the eighteenth century French tradition. Constructed with brick walls and cement stucco facing, its formal appearance derives from a central entrance pavilion and symmetrically placed wings. A hipped slate roof shelters a third floor defined by identical arched dormers on either side of a central pedimented bay that projects slightly forward from the entrance facade. The crowning pediment is decorated with dentil molding and features a central bullseye window with a ribbon and garland surround. The facades are quite plain, consisting of unadorned surfaces on the upper floor and panelling below the windows on both floors. Stone-like quoins at the corners of the building and at the corners of the central pavilion add architectural distinction to the facing. Large six-paned rectangular windows are used throughout the main floors, the ones on the ground floor slightly taller by the addition of upper arched transoms. Ground floor windows and doors are embellished by scrollwork keystones. The entrance door and the French doors leading out to terraces at the rear and side of house are adorned with scallop shell reliefs above these scrollwork keystones. These scallop details influenced the recent design of an emblem for the Bloedel Reserve. French doors at the front and rear of the second floor lead onto ornate wrought iron balconies that have the appearance of being supported by scrollwork corbels. The balcony at the rear extends across the entire central pavilion of the house—the former bedroom suite of Mrs. Collins that now provides offices for the Reserve. Similar wrought iron provides the principal decorative richness of the spiral staircase railing in the central entrance foyer.

The maid's quarters and kitchen areas of the house were contained in a two-story wing attached to the main house. As with the principal facades, this secondary wing is defined by a central doorway with windows on either side at the ground floor. Above, three arched dormer windows cut into the sloping roof.

Architect Jean Courtonne's 1720 design for a Parisian townhouse for the Noirmontier family. The symmetry, corner quoins, pediment, segmental arches, and wrought iron balconies of this eighteenth century type are reflected in Holmes's design of Collinswood.

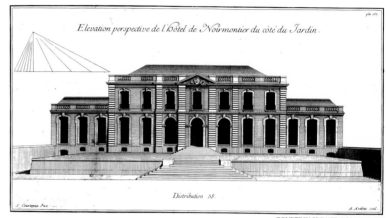

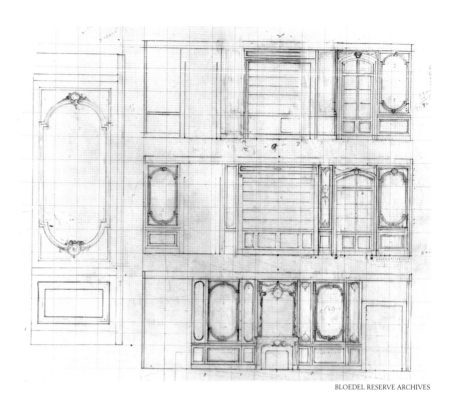

Sketches by Bertie Collins for a French country house suggested ornate panel moulding for the drawing room and library walls and ceiling The front elevation of the central pavilion showed ornate wrought iron balconies, an elaborate garland and scroll design for the pediment, and proposed urns and balustrade along the parapet

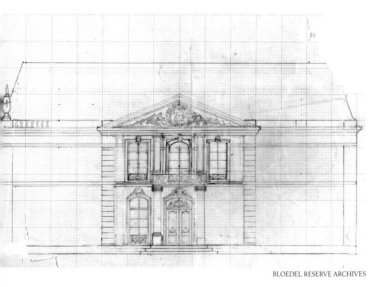

The house plans were ambitious, and certainly many degrees more elaborate than the rambling wooden hunting lodge at the water's edge. The beautifully proportioned drawing room north of the entrance hall had access from French doors to a terrace. The adjoining library and dining rooms were placed at the back of the house so the Collins family could take pleasure in the views of water and mountains. Upstairs were five bedrooms and three baths, plenty of room for Mrs. Collins to share with her children and grandchildren. The generous maid's quarters in the attached wing were reached from separate stairs and provided two bedrooms, a bathroom, and a central sitting room.

While the plans may have been grand, the money was in short supply in the years following the stock market crash of 1929. Bertie had envisioned a French chateau in an ornate style, with elaborate exterior decoration and richly carved panelling and fireplace mantels in the major rooms of the main floor. Bertie's extant sketches for the wall panelling, ceiling decorations, and library shelves in the main rooms are rich in rococo borders and ornament. He planned a very elaborate forecourt with garages and other subsidiary structures in

Clearing the woods on the bluff for the Collins house, 1930.

Construction proceeds, 1931.

the style of the main house. Baroque gardens were envisioned for the east and north sides of the house, with staircases and ramps descending the slopes. The rear terrace was to have been edged with a formal balustrade according to the rendering of the house and grounds prepared by well-known artist Norman Fox in 1930.

As architect Holmes recalled in a 1977 narrative:

The year 1930 brought some indication of cost care during the working drawing preparation stage. In the spring of thirty-one, it was decided to proceed. There were but few builders living on the Island and none seemed to be qualified for the project. Finally, a capable and energetic firm operating in Seattle and environs was engaged and since excavation equipment was not available on the Island, he dramatically delivered horses in a truck to prepare the site and to excavate for the basement area. Work on the super-structure followed and proceeded rapidly. A brother of the General Contractor operated the best millwork shop in Seattle and other

sub-contractors were equally qualified. During construction, Bertie often accompanied the architect to the site on the ferry, creating a close relationship with the owner and family and affording an exchange of experience and tales at home and abroad which were amusing to both.

By 1932, the house was complete, its exterior and interior finished more simply then originally planned, probably with the hope that as time went on, work could be completed as originally intended. Mrs. Collins's step-grandaughter recalls that the house, built as a year-round residence, was beautifully furnished but that her grand-mother rarely used the house in winter, preferring to be in town in the five-story Victorian home "with tapes-tried walls and a wonderful stairway" that took up a full square block of property at 702 Minor Avenue. This residence had been built for Seattle pioneer T.T. Minor and sold to John Collins in 1889. Mrs. Collins continued to come to Bainbridge during the summers until she became too ill; toward the end of her life, she was bedridden much of the time.

View of the apple orchard below the house on the bluff, 1935.

Although a formal garden was never realized for the property, Mrs. Collins did oversee a small garden adjoining the house. At the edge of the lawn on the north side of the house was a border with old-fashioned flowers and shrubs. Box pyramids were placed in the beds flanking the front door and at the side of the drive about halfway between the house and the elm trees that Mrs. Younger recalls planting when she was an eight-year old girl. Two Empress trees given to Mrs. Collins by Jim Eddy, an important figure in Puget Sound shipbuilding, still flank the west façade. Rhododendrons that came from the Minor Avenue house were also planted under Mrs. Collins' supervision. Most were later moved to the Glen by Mrs. Bloedel. A horse chestnut tree was salvaged by Mrs. Collins when a main street in Seattle was being widened. At the top of the slope behind the house was a boxwood hedge that originally extended completely along the eastern perimeter of the lawn. Its origins were in the original Collins homestead at Second Avenue and James Street. While the 1889 fire had destroyed the house, the hedge surrounding the house survived. John Collins had the hedge dug up; eventually it was taken over to Bainbridge and transplanted to the bluff where some of it remains to complement new landscaping of the site.

Mrs. Collins and her grandson Charlie, 1935.

In the saddle between the coastal bluff and the base of the hill to the east of the house had been an orchard—according to Mrs. Younger, "an old, old orchard, very gnarled, really not attractive." In order to keep deer away, little sacks of mothballs and the lids of tin cans that would blow against each other were hung from these trees. "And I remember, even as a child, I saw a certain incongruity to having these strange objects on the orchard trees right in front of my grandmother's very beautiful home." A few of the old trees remained as late as 1975.

Perspective of Reserve alterations to provide a workshop and garages, J. Lister Holmes, ca.1951

Workmen ponder what to do about the oil truck after the bridge collapses.

The property was entered from the county road through a pair of square gate piers surmounted by urns and supporting a wrought iron overthrow. A drive led through the second-growth forest to the main house. A bridge crossed the head of the main creek. An oil truck fell through the bridge in the late 1940s and in 1954 an earth dam replaced the bridge. In the process, a small pond was created on the uphill or west side. This is now the lower Swan Pond.

After acquiring the property in 1951, the Bloedels hired J. Lister Holmes to make alterations to the interior spaces and to design a three-car garage, storage, and workshop space for the family. At that time and shortly thereafter, Holmes rethought some of the original design

*The focal point of the entrance hall is a spiral
staircase with wrought iron baluster.*

ideas for the interior and modified them to accommodate panelling and bookshelves in the drawing room,
library, and dining room, and to modernize the kitchen
and service wing and the dressing rooms, baths, and
bedrooms upstairs. The one-story 1700-square-foot addition adjacent to the service wing went through a number
of design studies ranging in style from stark modernism
to compromise traditional. The client and the architect
reached a decision to go ahead with the latter, a low,
understated building faced with the same grey-tone
cement stucco and repeating the stone-like quoins in
corners and pillars. The stark blank walls have been
softened with an espalier apple tree and shrubs planted
in the French manner.

CHAPTER 3

GARDENS IN THE FOREST

The Bloedels in the Northwest

It was in some ways quite fitting that the Bloedels should purchase the Collins property, a site that had been logged to provide lumber and income for the Territorial University. The Bloedel name had been associated with the lumber industry in the Northwest since 1890. At that time, Julius Harold (J.H.) Bloedel, an engineering graduate of the University of Michigan and a native of Fond du Lac, Wisconsin, arrived in Bellingham and began what was to become a lifetime of work in the timber industry. In 1898, the same year he married, he organized the Lake Whatcom Logging Company. In 1911, Bloedel formed a partnership with railway contractors Patrick Welch and John W. Stewart that resulted in a lucrative purchase and logging of 10,000 acres of woodland in British Columbia near Myrtle Point on Vancouver Island. Operations eventually expanded to include other locations on the island. In 1913, Bloedel and his partner J. J. Donovan combined Lake Whatcom Logging Company with Larson Lumber Company and Bellingham Bay Mill Company to form the Bloedel-Donovan Lumber Mills. The company employed 2,000 workers in four sawmills, three shingle mills, a sash and door factory, and a box factory. In its time it was the largest mill on the West coast. Their efforts also opened up the Olympic Peninsula to logging. When this company was liquidated in 1945, J.H. Bloedel became chairman of the board of two companies, the Columbia Valley Lumber Company (considered the successor to Bloedel-Donovan) and Bloedel, Stewart and Welch, Ltd. of British Columbia. As the business grew in size and success, a sales office opened in Seattle with branch offices in New York and Chicago.

In 1911, Bloedel relocated his wife, Mina, and their three children, Lawrence, Prentice, and Charlotte, from Bellingham to Seattle. They moved three times in seven years before settling into a commodious English-style

home at 1137 Harvard Avenue East. This residence had been designed by Seattle architect Carl Gould and built for Francis Brownell. As with many fashionable Seattle homes, this one became available when Brownell moved to the exclusive Highlands area north of the city by 1918.

The family of R.D. Merrill resided in the next block at 919 Harvard Avenue East. A fourth-generation member of a lumber dynasty, he had come west from Saginaw, Michigan in the last decade of the nineteenth century. His initial land purchases were in the Aberdeen area and on Vancouver Island. Merrill's home was an elegant neoclassical building designed by famed New York architect and landscape architect Charles Adams Platt in 1909. Platt also selected furnishings in Europe and created a beautiful Italian Renaissance-style garden for the property. The elder daughter, Virginia, grew up in

Camellia

The formal garden of the R. D. Merrill home in 1913.

a very different social atmosphere than did her husband-to-be, Prentice Bloedel. According to the recollection of Virginia Wright, the Bloedels' elder daughter, the Merrill environment was "jolly, expansive, sociable, and gregarious" in contrast to the formality of the Bloedel home. She recalls Mina Bloedel as quite fastidious and strict. J.H. was autocratic, at least during his later years when she was growing up and attending family get-togethers.

Despite the geographic closeness of the two families and the lumber businesses that each ran, there appears to have been little social interaction between the Merrills and the Bloedels. Perhaps this was because the Bloedels were newer to Seattle and didn't entertain to any great extent. Also, J. H. was continually working out-of-town to build his company. In contrast, the Merrills had settled in Seattle earlier and were well established financially and socially in the community. They were friends with the Joshua Greens and other Seattle first families.

Prentice Bloedel had attended Thacher School in California and gone east to college at Yale University. He had returned to Thacher to teach geometry and trigonometry for a year. He had also worked as a laborer for three months at Lake Whatcom before being stricken with poliomyelitis. Three years of recuperation and a year at the Harvard Business School followed during which he formulated a desire to study engineering and inventing—clearly not the career his father had in mind for his eldest son. In 1927 he married Virginia Merrill. They settled in Williamstown, Massachussetts where his younger brother Lawrence also lived, having managed to maintain distance from the company and remain in academic circles in the Northeast. But pressure from his father and his new wife and a strongly instilled sense of family obligation moved Prentice Bloedel to Vancouver in 1929, where he began work at the Bloedel, Stewart and Welch head office on West Hastings Street. In *Empire of Wood, the MacMillan Bloedel Story*, Donald MacKay says, "he was prepared to follow his father's wishes in the tradition of lumber families imbued with a sense of dynasty."

Despite Prentice's initial misgivings, the lumber business came to have a special meaning to him as he became more involved with the company. As his daughter, Virginia Wright, describes it, he developed an almost mystical or religious feeling for land—for its ownership, the livelihood it provided, and the responsibility people had to conserve and protect it for future generations. He put this philosophy into action in the 1940s when he bought huge amounts of cut-over land in Whatcom County and began a reforestation program. These lands formed the basis of what later became Bloedel Timberlands Development Company, which today operates over 50,000 acres of tree farms in Washington and Alabama.

In 1942, Prentice Bloedel became president and treasurer of the Canadian firm. The following year, Bloedel-Donovan Mills phased out its operations. J. H. Bloedel remained chairman of the Columbia Valley Company and Bloedel, Stewart and Welch. In 1950, Prentice Bloedel initiated negotiations to merge Bloedel, Stewart and Welch with H. R. MacMillan Export Company, its chief competitor. As his last act before retiring, J. H. Bloedel signed the documents of amalgamation in October, 1951. To Prentice, his father

> … was not a complicated man, but a wonderful man, and took a prominent place in the industry. He was strong. He pioneered the shipping of lumber from Washington to the Atlantic coast by sea. But really his business philosophy was to own timber. It was a passion that dominated all his life, and as a result he became a sawmill man.

The merger created MacMillan and Bloedel Limited, the largest lumber and pulp company in British Columbia. Prentice became one of two vice-chairmen, a position he himself devalued, "I had no function whatever as vice-chairman, but of course I did have a voice in the executive committee and expressed myself." With the merger, the Bloedel holdings included Bloedel Timberlands Development, Inc., Columbia Valley Lumber Company in Bellingham, and MacMillan Bloedel, Ltd. of Vancouver, B.C. Within two years of the merger, Prentice and Virginia Bloedel left Vancouver, B.C. permanently to move to Collinswood on Bainbridge Island.

COURTESY VIRGINIA WRIGHT

COURTESY VIRGINIA WRIGHT

J. H. and young Prentice Bloedel in the early 1920s.

Prentice and Virginia Bloedel shortly before their marriage, 1927.

40

EASTERN FRONT OF COLLINSWOOD NEAR SEATTLE, WASH.

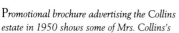

Settlement of an estate now makes available one of the fine residential properties of the Puget Sound area. "Collinswood" is a charming, 15-room modern home on Bainbridge Island, 8 miles from the City of Seattle.

Collinswood stands on a beautifully landscaped knoll overlooking Puget Sound, with the Cascade Mountains in the background. A private, fine sandy beach fronts the property on the salt waters of the Sound.

This is an exceptional opportunity to buy reasonably a lovely, spacious family home in a setting of striking beauty—a green wonderland of scenic pleasure the year around. Here is restful quiet with every convenience and recreational facility of modern living.

BLOEDEL RESERVE ARCHIVES

Promotional brochure advertising the Collins estate in 1950 shows some of Mrs. Collins's prized rhododendron collection, most of which is now located in The Glen.

Agate Point Farm

The Merrill family had a summer home also designed by Charles Platt. Mrs. Bloedel and her daughters, Virginia and Eulalie, spent summers at Restoration Point, 'The Country Club' at the southern end of Bainbridge Island. Prentice meanwhile occupied himself with the business in Vancouver and came down on weekends and in September. He enjoyed being on Bainbridge Island and hoped eventually to own his own country place. When the Bloedels were considering moving back to Seattle after the merger, they discussed living in the city, building a house on property owned by R. D. Merrill in The Highlands, or finding property on Bainbridge Island. As it happened, the Collins estate was on the market—empty for years. Mrs. Bloedel had known both Mrs. Collins and her son Bertie. Her attraction to the Collins house was tied somewhat to the way in which it recalled the symmetry and formality of the family home in Seattle. But it probably had more to do with her own taste. She had developed an appreciation for eighteenth-century French interior design, and had filled their Tudor house in Vancouver with French furniture and accessories. She was quite naturally drawn to the Lister Holmes house since it corresponded with her taste for French decor.

While they had both travelled in France and had found the chateau country to be a great experience, the most vivid architectural memories the Bloedels recalled dated from a trip they had taken to Scandinavia in the 1930s to look at pulp mills being built there that might be the model for a pulp mill in Port Alberni. They visited an estate on the outskirts of Stockholm that impressed

them, particularly the fact that the house walls "came straight down to the ground, with no gardening around it — you see the base of the house as it hits the ground." That idea was interesting to them. When they saw the Collins house years later, they would recall the Scandinavian manor house. Here again was a formal villa, the walls of which "came right out of the ground, with no softening." They decided to purchase the property and re-named it Agate Point Farm.

The drawing room. Gilt mirrors flank the marble fireplace, above which is a painting by Henri Matisse.

Hesselby, an estate near Stockholm, greatly impressed the Bloedels during their travels.

MARY RANDLETT

Mrs. Bloedel with daughters Virginia (left) and Eulalie (right) in the drawing room at the Reserve, 1967. Painting above the sofa is by Eduard Vuillard.

RICHARD BROWN

Although Mrs. Bloedel was not an active gardener, she had grown up in the surroundings of the formal gardens at 919 Harvard East, designed in the tradition of seventeenth-century Italian gardens. Her mother had been one of the early members of the Seattle Garden Club and had taken a strong interest in civic projects and beautification. While the Vancouver home had a modest garden in which she took only a passing interest, Mrs. Bloedel initially knew more about horticulture than Prentice and was more interested in specific plants and flowers. Her taste at the Reserve is expressed in the Rhododendron Glen, the Ravine, the candelabra primulas, ginger, cyclamen, oxalis and other wildflowers on the property.

For Prentice, the house was secondary in importance to the land itself. His daughter recalls how important it was to him to own this land and to develop it.

> I remember when they first got the property, Daddy used to go out every day with his machete, carving paths through the place. He really loved to explore this property, get to know it and feel it and find out about it. He would insist on taking us kids around. Now I could think of nothing more boring than getting all cut up in the brambles. But he really would struggle around every day it seemed and for him with that polio it was quite a hike because it wasn't easy for him to get around. But for him, having that land to understand and explore and develop was similar to an artist having a canvas. He found this was a real opportunity that realized a lot of imagination and creativity in him.

Prentice Bloedel had long been actively engaged in the growing and managing of stands of second-growth timber. His interest in conservation was expressed in an address he delivered to the annual banquet of the University of Washington Forest Club and College of Forestry Alumni Association on March 5, 1955.

> [Conservation] is a way of thinking that is just being formed, and so, if it is to have any real meaning for us as a nation, its shape will be hammered out by all of us, emerging, not tomorrow as a completed figure, but formed over the years by the thoughts and actions of many. It seems to me that, like all great forward steps, the first glimpse of truth comes to the world from a poet or a dreamer. The banner is snatched away by a band of devoted and enthusiastic followers, and the movement is launched on a great wave of emotion. But as time goes on, the movement becomes the property of everyone. It is assimilated, its significance probed, and the original poetic concept is worked into the practical tool of everyday life.

The dining room's French provincial furnishings are set off by Aubusson carpet. Over the fireplace is an oil painting by late nineteenth century French artist Berthe Morisot.

The library, with its Venetian glass chandelier, 1982. Above the desk is a painting by Northwest artist Morris Graves.

MARY RANDLETT

MARY RANDLETT

*Prentice and Virginia Bloedel enjoy
a restful moment at the Reserve,
August 1967.*

In retrospect, his general remarks concerning conservation figure in his conceptual work on the gardens at his Bainbridge Island home—the poet and dreamer creating from the wilderness a place perfectly suited to the appreciation of the natural world, both in its wildness and in its more tamed image.

In an article written for the University of Washington Arboretum Bulletin in Spring 1980, Prentice Bloedel discussed the purpose and future of the Reserve as he saw it. In doing so, he also described the house and grounds as he and his wife Virginia found them when they acquired the property in 1951 and the impression that it made upon them.

> With the exception of a tiny garden around the house the whole property was covered with a young mixed conifer hardwood stand, two streams, swamps and brushy patches typical of so much cutover forest land in the Pacific Northwest. In spite of our citified pasts it wasn't long before we were exploring the old logging roads that threaded the woods, heading out cross country to see what we could find, following fence lines. In the course of these forays we found the land itself marvellously varied in contour and physiography. We found single plants and colonies of fragile woodland species, mosses, ferns, a world of incomparable diversity, a panorama of survival in an eternal struggle, exciting in its vitality. We found that plants often have a way of arranging and disposing themselves with a harmony of color, texture and form when left to themselves. We discovered that there is grandeur in decay; the rotten log hosting seedlings of hemlocks, cedars, huckleberries, the shape of a crumbling snag.

> Out of these experiences comes an unexpected insight. Respect for trees and plants replaces indifference; one feels the existence of a divine order. Man is not set apart from the rest of nature—he is just a member of that incredibly diverse population of the universe, a member that nature can do without but who cannot do without nature. One realizes that we humans are trustees in this world, that our power should be exercised in this context.

RICHARD BROWN

This new awareness determined us to set the land aside for the primary purpose of providing others with the opportunity to enjoy plants both as arranged by man and as they arrange themselves; and for the purpose of providing people wandering about the Reserve a refreshing experience of nature and a broadening of their appreciation of their world.

C H A P T E R   4

THE DREAM REALIZED

*We are finding, as perhaps some of you have done, that it is
one thing to see the vision, another to capture it with sticks
and stones. Once, long ago when we were starting to carve
the large pool in front of the house out of an alder swamp,
Thomas Church, the California landscape architect who
was helping us then, said, 'I admire your courage.' His
remark was not intended as a compliment. It was a kindly
way of saying, 'have you bitten off more than you can
chew?' It didn't register particularly at the time; it does
now.*

from *"The Bloedel Reserve—Its Purpose , Its Future,"* U.W.
Arboretum Bulletin, Spring 1980

  It is fair to say that up until the Arbor Fund hired
Environmental Planning and Design of Pittsburgh in
1986, there had been no overview prepared for the
Reserve. Instead, for nearly 30 years, Prentice Bloedel's
personal exploration of various ideas, either his own or
those inspired by his exposure to gardens during his
travels or his reading, provided the vision for work at the
Reserve. During that period, the gardens of the old
Collinswood estate took shape in small increments with
little or no master planning. Instead, the property became
a canvas for experimentation of various concepts that
either pleased or displeased the owners. Their taste in
landscape evolved over time. Bloedel requested or
received ideas from some of the finest designers in the
field and took or rejected whole or partial concepts as he
decided they might suit the character of the property.
Generally the conflicts revolved about the formality of
many of the design solutions, most of which were at odds
with the Bloedels' desires to reinforce and embellish the
natural qualities of the Reserve and avoid designs that
were pretentious or dominating. Looking at the proposals from 1951 through 1985 the reader can appreciate
the wealth of concepts the Bloedels initiated and how
many designers and skilled workers were called upon to
provide these ideas and implement some of them.

The Inheritance

  Otto Holmdahl was the first of a long line of
designers who worked for the Bloedels. Prentice Bloedel
remembers that he and his wife "inherited" the Swedish
landscape designer who had been the landscape advisor
to Mrs. Collins. Holmdahl had an extensive practice in
Seattle and Tacoma from the early 1920s until his death
in the early 1960s. He designed many of the largest and
most important gardens in Puget Sound. One of the best
preserved of his designs is the garden of William Boeing Jr.
in the Highlands. Holmdahl was one of the first professional landscape designers in the Northwest to cele-
brate the use of native plants. He was also known for

Primula

MARY RANDLETT

This rooster, for thirty years the greeter at the gates of Agate Point Farm, now welcomes guests to the Bloedel Reserve.

his skill in the use of poured concrete to simulate natural rocks and for retaining large tree stumps as features in his gardens. A notable example of the former is the old bear grotto at the Woodland Park Zoo, which is now part of the gorilla exhibit. Holmdahl was also the original landscape architect at Seattle Center, but died before the completion of the World's Fair in 1962.

For the Bloedels, Holmdahl prepared a scheme for the gardens around the house. He envisioned the creation of a large, wide flight of stairs down the eastern hill slope and a formal hedge facing the house beyond the central lawn panel of the motor court. He also proposed planting several small trees. The formality of his plan was not in keeping with the Bloedels' wish for more naturalistic landscaping. Their disagreement over this landscape treatment led to the dissolution of the contract. As Mr. Bloedel put it, "we found that he was too set in his ways" to work with them.

As part of the architectural work done to modernize the house in September of 1952, plans were prepared for a retaining wall on the south and west sides of the motor court. Although the plans did not show a flight of stairs in the corner, they were eventually built. Also during this year, the Bloedels had the monumental gate piers at the entrance to the property moved to the south several feet to serve as the entrance to the farm road. Holes were dug and the pillars were partially buried to form simpler, smaller gateposts. A low stone wall and wood entrance gates were installed, the scale more in keeping with rural country homes than the chateau ambiance the earlier gates had embodied. Shortly thereafter, a pine grove was planted at the entrance and along the old north drive.

One of the earliest landscape projects on the property was the building of an earth dam in the location where a section of the old road had collapsed under the weight of an oil delivery truck. The Swan Pond and Waterfall, constructed by Ray Prentice of Prentice Nursery in Seattle, were by-products of this new dam. During the 1950s, largely because of the interest and

PROPOSED·WEST TERRACE

Thomas Church did this perspective view of the north terrace (incorrectly referred to as the west terrace) in September, 1955. It shows the proposed staircase and rock wall above Rhododendron Glen.

persistence of Mrs. Bloedel, the area to the north and around the dam was transformed into a rhododendron glen complete with waterfall, plantings, and trails. While she herself did none of the work, she was very interested in wildflowers; she supervised the gardeners, selected plant materials, and diligently added to the collection.

A Friendship with Thomas Church

In August 1954, seeking to explore the possibility of creating a pond from the alder swamp west of the house, the Bloedels began a long and amicable relationship with the well-known landscape architect Thomas Church of San Francisco. They had first heard about him from a Vancouver friend, Kay Benoist, who had married

the head of Almaden Vintners and had moved to the Bay area. The Bloedels brought Church to Seattle to consult on one of a number of projects they were then considering for the property. To Bloedel's eye, Church's concepts were "too manipulative," as he put it, "too much architecture, too little nature." Nevertheless, they became fast friends and Church informally advised them for many years, offering ideas and criticism. The arrival of Church each year was the impetus for festive social gatherings. It was probably during one of his yearly visits that Mrs. Corydon Wagner, Virginia Bloedel's sister, met Church and his wife. They became friends and Eulalie hired him to work on the design of her garden 'Lakewold' near Tacoma. Like the Reserve, it also will be a public garden at some point in the future.

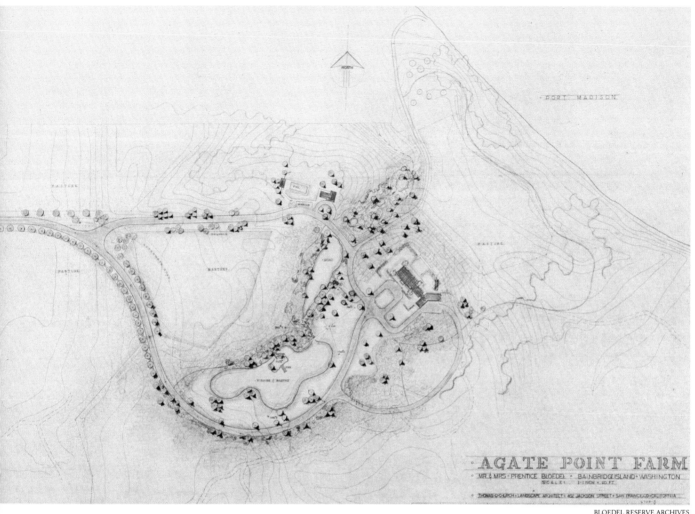

In his 1955 plan drawing of Agate Point Farm, Thomas Church promoted active recreation – a pond for boating and fishing surrounded by a golf course.

Of all the professionals with whom the Bloedels consulted, Church was the most prestigious. A landscape architect of national stature, Church had been educated at the University of California, Berkeley and at Harvard. Upon graduation, he had travelled extensively in Europe studying the application of historic garden traditions, especially of the Mediterranean Basin, to California conditions. He opened his practice in the San Francisco Bay area at the beginning of the Depression. His work in the 1930s reflected a progressive and gradual simplification of historic styles in garden design, particularly Italian Renaissance, French Baroque, and Spanish, that culminated in a completely abstract idiom that contained some of the earliest Modern landscape designs in the United States. He used plants for their design qualities, treating them as sculptural elements or abstract walls or planes on the ground. His practice was almost entirely residential, although he was the consulting landscape architect at the university campuses at Berkeley, Stanford, and Santa Cruz. Between 1939 and 1955, his office was an atelier as well, attracting young designers eager to learn from Church.

In his role as a counselor and advisor to the Bloedels, Church prepared a number of conceptual drawings for various parts of the Reserve. He proposed the creation of the largest of the ponds and a new drive to the south of the pond which, together with the existing drive, form the scenic loop that is in place today. He suggested a small island in the new pond, to be surrounded by a five-hole golf course. The latter existed into the 1970s; the former became one of many uninitiated projects.

On the north side of the original entrance drive, roughly at the head of Rhododendron Glen, Church proposed a guesthouse and a swimming pool. From the time of their return to Seattle, the Bloedels had frequently entertained Vancouver friends on the weekends. The guesthouse was seen as a place apart for these visitors as well as a place for Bagley and Virginia Wright and their children on their frequent visits. But Church's location did not suit the Bloedels and it was several years later that they selected the existing site at the head of the chain of lakes.

In 1956, the Bloedels hired Fujitaro Kubota to create a garden in the Japanese style and gave him a great deal of leeway in its composition. No drawings or plans exist from that effort because Kubota preferred to work by moving and placing the plant materials, rocks, and design elements in the landscape until he saw them exactly where he wanted them. He would sit on a little stool and direct his two sons in the moving of garden elements. He was a small man and his sons towered above him. Nevertheless, Mr. Bloedel recalls that when he spoke, they jumped!

RICHARD BROWN

MARY RANDLETT

RICHARD BROWN

MARY RANDLETT

Fujitaro Kubota had emigrated from Japan to San Francisco in 1906, later settling in Seattle, where he and his family operated the Taft Hotel. During this time, Kubota developed his skills and interests in gardening and, by 1923, he had decided to turn his hobby into a full-time profession as one of Seattle's first Japanese gardeners. Some of his most notable work included the Rainier Club and parts of Seattle University, as well as many larger homes in Magnolia, Laurelhurst, and Windermere. In 1929, he selected a site in south Seattle that, over the course of the next fifty years, he developed into display gardens borrowing freely from the Japanese tradition and American garden concepts. The Kubota family business evolved from a plant and lawn maintenance enterprise initially to encompass landscape design, instal-

lation, and construction. Their Seattle garden grew with waterfalls, ponds, bridges, stone and concrete. Mr. Bloedel hired him on the basis of his work locally in the Japanese-American garden idiom.

At the suggestion of Thomas Church, Paul Hayden Kirk was hired in 1960 to create a guesthouse overlooking Kubota's garden. This was in the area south and west of that originally proposed by Church. Taking his cue from the Japanese garden, Kirk designed a building that has elements tying it to Japanese temple architecture. It also subtly suggests Northwest Coast Indian longhouses. Kirk's beautifully detailed Northwest contemporary residence combines glass and native woods to blend harmoniously with the surroundings.

Weeping cut-leaf maple in the Japanese Garden frames this view to the guesthouse.

Close-up of wood post and siding at the guesthouse.

54

View of guesthouse and Zen garden

Guesthouse and swimming pool viewed from top of the blue fescue mound, 1981.

The guesthouse is built of vertical grain western red cedar with Douglas fir posts. It includes a basement containing rest rooms — once the dressing rooms for the pool that originally was adjacent to the building — and a main floor consisting of a large living/dining area, two bedrooms, two bathrooms, and a small kitchen area. The step-down living area features a tile hearth with a chimney that soars upward through the two-story high central A frame. This room is defined by open beams supporting a sharply pitched glass skylight running the length of the central axis. Floor-to-ceiling windowed bays with sliding shoji screens form most of the exterior side walls. Above these glass and wood frames, gray colored board with wood verticals embellishes the façade. The exterior ends are of narrow, horizontal cedar plank panelling. At either end of the building, four triangles of clear glass form a large triangular face that, along with the central axis skylight, bathes the teak-floored central room in natural light. The rectangular building is surrounded by a generous hexagonal frame deck composed of clear Alaska yellow cedar with simple cedar railings and built-in wood seating overlooking the Japanese garden and pond. The wooden posts below the deck have uplift crossbars. Taking cues from Japanese roofing, the ridge beam at the apex of the skylight terminates in uplifted ends, as do the terminating horizontals of the deck railing. To the north of the guesthouse, a swimming pool was installed that in later years became the site of the controversial Garden of Planes.

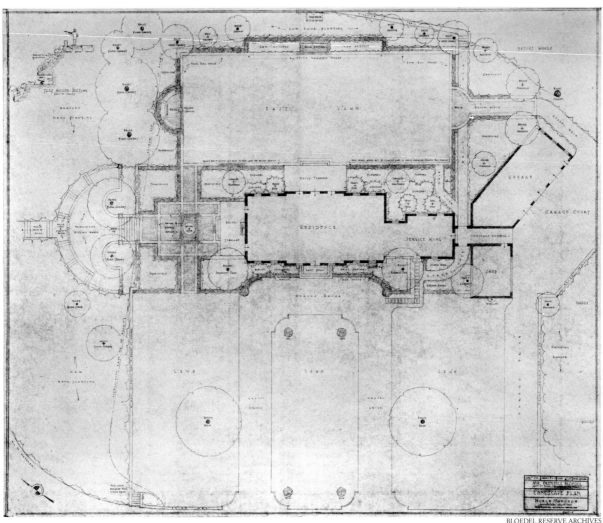

Landscape plan by Noble Hoggson dated July 16, 1956 showed formal north terrace similar to – although simpler than – that suggested by Thomas Church, with brick and pebble mosaics and brick walled terrace on east lawn.

In a revised landscape study dated May 10, 1956, Church suggested that the east side of the house lead to a brick paved promenade with a north/south axis defined by crisscrossing boxwood hedges to complement the extant north/south boxwood hedge. Grass lawns were on either side of the court. For the north side of the house, another formal terrace was paved with exposed aggregate and brick geometric pavers. The focus of this terrace was a symmetrical curving double staircase.

The areas immediately adjoining the main house received a great deal of attention from the 1950s well into the 1980s. A great many formal and informal plans were formulated, rethought, and put aside as the Bloedels sought out simpler, more subtle solutions. In January 1955, Church prepared two schemes for the area to the east of the house. Both concepts were for formal gardens with a paved area centered on the house and extending out as far as the boxwood hedge. Church contemplated a somewhat free treatment of the southern end of the east lawn adjacent to the garage wing. In September of that year, he presented a scheme for the bank north of the house – a central flight of stairs leading to a large semicircular platform. Not unlike some of the ideas Bertie Collins

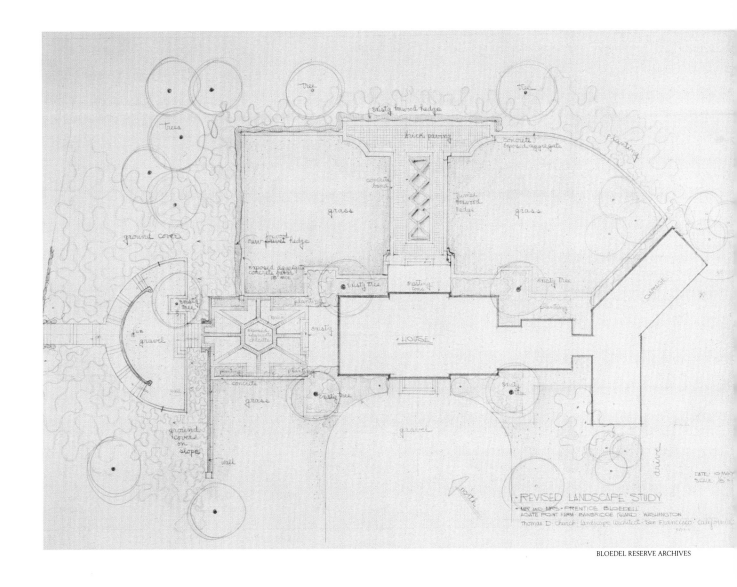

suggested, or the garden and stairway designs J. Lister Holmes would have prepared for such a house, these plans nevertheless were too elaborate and formal for the Bloedels, whose emerging taste was for simplicity and the primacy of landscape over built objects.

In July of the following year, landscape architect Noble Hoggson prepared two designs for the east, north, and west gardens surrounding the house. Hoggson had been trained at Harvard in the late 1920s. He is best known in Seattle for his plans for the west garden at the Seattle Art Museum in Volunteer Park. According to Bloedel, Hoggson came to the Reserve once a week "to advise." In one of the Reserve drawings, he indicated that the paving design was to be provided by Thomas Church.

By October, Church himself had provided the Bloedels with a scheme for the north bank in a plan almost identical to that of the Hoggson scheme. The detailing, however, was typical of work that he was currently doing in gardens in the San Francisco Bay Peninsula.

In 1967 and again in 1970, Church designed schemes for formal terraces for the north bank, neither of which were executed. He also submitted sketches for formal stairs on the east bank. Finally, in 1974, one of his suggested treatments of the east bank — a simple over-look — was executed. It was a far cry from the elaborate proposals for formal stairways, terraces and parterres he had presented over the course of twenty years. It was also the last project Church undertook for the Bloedels.

58

THE PROBLEM: a long rectangular pool set in an alder grove. space leaks out in several directions — lack of focus. or adequate edge. Pool set flush with ground but water level below edge of ground — benches of wood sections of arcs. Sense of awkwardness as it exists

Needed: Either greater contrast between geometry and looseness of nature or more integration — Better definition of the space as an exterior room.

Excerpt from notes made in October 1970 for Mr. Bloedel's Pond by Laurie Olin entitled, "Suggestions on a dilemma."

Finnish and English canal ponds. Whereas these ponds had running water, Mr. Bloedel likened his reflection pool to them because it was fed by a natural spring, not artificially by pipes, as is the case with most still ponds. Church developed this concept at a place where a spring bubbled up in the woods. By 1970, it had been taken to the stage of engineering drawings by the Seattle firm of Skelling, Helle, Christianson and Robertson. Church suggested that since the area had a very high water table, an ornamental pool could be formed by simply placing a curb in the wet ground and grading the bottom of the pool so that it would fill from the bottom. He suggested the dimensions of the pool, and the engineers laid out the curbing, pool bottom, and drainage system for it. Later in that year, a series of studies by Laurie Olin, then in the office of landscape architect Richard Haag, suggested several alterations to the pool to include the use of sculpture, a structure, or raised curbs that formed walls. Daughter Virginia herself initiated the idea of a sculptural focus for the pool. None of these treatments was endorsed by the Bloedels, whose preference was toward meditation without the intrusion of objects that might take away from the general ambiance of the site. Simple benches and English yew hedges surrounding the pool were considered by Bloedel and by Richard Haag. The final selection of Irish yew hedges was made by the Bloedels, who personally travelled to Portland, Oregon to purchase plants of sufficient quality and age. Haag recommended that the woodland side of the hedge grow naturally, in contrast to the trimmed inner face — a suggestion that has not been followed.

Management Changes

In 1970, the Bloedels deeded the Reserve property to the University of Washington with restrictions placed upon its maintenance and use. The decision to donate the land and its improvements was based on the perception that the Reserve might not survive as a private entity. The University could assure its preservation and could see to it that it was set aside for the benefit of

Church was particularly fond of the area between the Swan Pond and the guesthouse in the Douglas firs, and it was his suggestion that a trail be placed between the trees. In August 1957, Church prepared a diagrammatic tree planting scheme for the area now referred to as the Orchid Walk — earlier known as Church Walk — and for the planting of ornamental trees on the south loop of the drive. The latter proposal was rejected, but in 1974 his proposal for the walk area was finally developed exactly as he had laid it out when he walked through the forest.

One other significant element of the Reserve owes its success to Church's skills. The reflection pool was inspired by photographs Prentice Bloedel had seen of

DICK BUSHER

Reflection Pool, 1982.

Reflection Pool before planting the hedge and turf

the public. In 1974, the Arbor Fund, a nonprofit foundation, was established and an endowment created to assure perpetual maintenance of the Reserve.

There had always been a fundamental difference in the goals of the University and those of the Bloedels for the property. The University's natural objective had been one of research and education. The Bloedels wanted to encourage public enjoyment of nature and were concerned that the gardens might be turned into a teaching arboretum. In 1985, having assured through endowment that the property could maintain itself without outside assistance, a mutually accommodating agreement was reached and the Arbor Fund bought the property back from the University of Washington.

RICHARD HAAG

Sheep in the south meadow, 1965.

Curatorial Care

In 1976, Richard Brown was hired as curator of the Reserve. Over the next ten years, he formed a close relationship with the Bloedels by working in proximity to their home, spending many hours walking with them through the grounds, and discussing the plans for the property. Bloedel respected Brown's honest evaluations of his ideas for the garden, and that respect formed the basis for a fair, open association. At least during the early years of Brown's tenure, Mr. Bloedel was thoroughly interested in the everyday work being done on the grounds. He stopped by Brown's office once or twice a day. Brown found him to be "a very clear thinking person, one who could look around a problem, come at it from perhaps more than one direction, a person who was very sensitive to details and to human issues."

The period during which Brown was brought to the Reserve was one of change. In particular, staffing

RICHARD BROWN

Swan cygnets six days old

Racoons romp through the Reserve grounds.

RICHARD BROWN

changes were being made to accommodate the future public role the Reserve would serve. When Brown arrived, the house was the Bloedels' home and the guesthouse was being used for entertaining family and out-of-town guests. The Bloedels at that time were focusing their energies on transplanting trees and shrubs and making minor trail alterations. To the south of the main gate, sheep grazed and there were steer in the west meadow near the barns.

This meadow became the testing ground for Brown in 1978. With an increasing workforce and expanding stockpile of equipment and supplies, one priority was the development of an adequate maintenance complex. Mr. Brown investigated other facilities and talked with crews about types of buildings at colleges and golf courses, which were comparable areas. A fairly elaborate maintenance building was in the planning stages when it was suggested that perhaps some of the existing barns south of the entrance could be converted. The suggestion was considered and approved, and Brown was given authority to supervise and manage the project without any intervention from Bloedel — a test of Brown's ability to administer and oversee a large-scale project. Jack Vincent and Associates was hired to design the remodeling of the eastern barn (one of two parallel barns on the site) to

house a crew area and storage for equipment, pesticides, and chemicals. Completed at a cost of $98,000, the remodelled barn and an adjacent pole structure for storage of hay and wood received Mr. Bloedel's approval and reaffirmed his confidence in Brown's capabilities.

During 1977-78, at the suggestion of Mr. Bloedel, Brown interviewed several young landscape architects to help develop conceptual plans for certain problematic areas on the grounds. He engaged Diane Steen, a recent graduate from the University of Washington. Her role was to convert Mr. Bloedel's descriptions and ideas to drawings that could be further refined and evaluated, and later installed. Few of these ideas were ever carried out. But one area took up a considerable amount of her time. The east bluff, the site of Mrs. Collins' crabapple orchard had, by 1978, become a focal point for concern. It was, in Brown's words,

a hodgepodge of plantings, an uninteresting site, a place of horticultural neglect. On the banks around the house were mass plantings of old shrubs left over from the Collins period. The bank to the right of the stairs to the Glen consisted of native huckleberries, snowberries, forsythia, fieldgrass, all unkept.

62

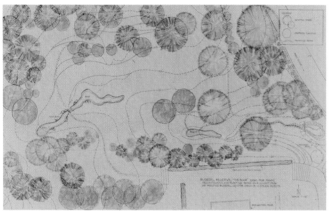

Proposed viewing terrace overlooking the sound shows bank cut and recontouring. Based on a sketch by Mr. Bloedel. Drawn by Diane Steen.

The Room — ideas for ponds, recontouring, and planting based on a concept from Mr. Prentice Bloedel. Drawn by Diane Steen.

Prentice Bloedel devised a conceptual scheme, refined by Diane Steen, that consisted of a formal pool flanked by large mounds. By 1980, this formal treatment had been rejected because of the lack of water in the area. Instead, it was regraded and planted as Richard Haag had suggested, first in wildflowers, then in grass as it remains today.

Diane Steen also prepared schemes for a pond in the south wood, use of the remaining farm buildings nearby, and one for an area to be called The Room that is currently the site of the Moss Garden or Anteroom. The overflow from the reflecting pond and drainage from the area west of it gathered into a streambed that led eastward (passing under the driveway through a culvert into a stream channel) to the Japanese pool. Although the upper streambed near the reflecting pond was quite handsome, the lower streambed, which could be seen from the driveway, was less pleasing. George Schenk, a rock garden enthusiast interested in native plant materials, suggested the term "the room," drawing the analogy of an actual room in "the building of the garden." Schenk prepared an elaborate plan that would call for the use of a considerable number of alpine and rock garden-type ground covers. Nothing came of his design for the site. Richard Yamasaki, brought in to do pruning work in the Japanese garden, proposed extending the ambiance of the Japanese garden up the stream through the use of appropriate plantings and the placement of handsome stones to create a dry streambed effect. This idea also failed to move Bloedel, who was always resistant to overmanipulating the specimens, particularly in disturbing the almost magical qualities of the forest in this section of the property. It awaited the arrival of Richard Haag for its ultimate transformation into the present garden.

Richard Haag

All these false starts and unsuccessful plans had their effect. It became clear that the property, if it was to grow and be shaped in a consistent manner, required a master plan. In 1978, the Bloedels held a competition for such a development plan. The process was well orchestrated by the Planning and Development Committee of the Arbor Fund, the nonprofit organization created in 1974 to manage the Reserve. The committee established a competition and invited four participants to submit proposals—Arthur Erickson, the Canadian architect; and three local firms; Grant Jones; Richard Haag; and Jongejan, Gerrard and McNeil. Each design firm was given the same four areas of the property to address in a two-month long master plan design effort. While others used aerial photography, slide programs, renderings, and overlays as part of their presentations, Richard Haag was the least formal and most spontaneous of the competitors, drawing freehand sketches of his concepts before the committee — Mr. Bloedel; his daughter, Virginia Wright; architect Paul Kirk; and Lee Copeland, professor at the University of Washington. They selected Haag because of his knowledge of plants, artistic skills, sensitivity to the owners' intent, and creativity. During the next seven years, Mr. Bloedel and Richard Haag worked incrementally on sub-areas of the property in a fashion that was effective but still far less systematic and planned than the Arbor Fund had envisioned.

Richard Haag had spent most of his life among plants. His early years were spent in and around his father's nursery in Kentucky. It was not surprising that while still a child he developed a penchant for growing things and exploring the possibilities of hybrids. After attending school at the universities of Illinois, Berkeley, and Harvard, Haag went to work for San Francisco landscape architect Lawrence Halprin, later opening his own private practice in the Bay area. Relocating to Seattle, Haag taught courses in landscape architecture at the University of Washington and founded the Department of Landscape Architecture there. He maintained a private practice that branched out from residential work into broader fields. In 1962, he was responsible for transforming the site of the Seattle World's Fair into a city park. His shaping of the grounds at the Battelle Seattle Research Centers demonstrated a sensitive and harmonious blending of native plantings, wild shrubs, and manicured lawn areas. His most significant project, Gasworks Park, received the President's Honor Award from the American Society of Landscape Architects for its innovative reclamation of a hazardous industrial area for city parkland.

During 1980, Mr. Haag proposed a series of small dams on the north creek in the Rhododendron Glen. Two pools were built and his plans for regrading the orchard area and for replanting of the north bank near the house were carried out. The waterfront bluff had always been a visual distraction. Haag suggested dropping the edge of the bluff approximately 25 feet. Two mounds were left at nearly the original height of the bluff —all the rest was excavated and removed and a trapezoidal wedge of sheep fescue was planted. Haag thought it would cause the viewer's eye to flow across the bluff to the water, which was perceived to be the focal point. On the outer flanks of the fescue would be a colorful display of wildflowers.

The concept was an attractive one. Unfortunately, it failed to produce the desired effect. The Reserve had decided against soil sterilization as a means for weed control and had not counted on the clover and perennial orchard grasses taking over and dwarfing the shorter fescue. It was impossible to weed out the more common grasses. The site also lacked irrigation, and the quality of topsoil was variable. By summer, the effort was recognized as a "disaster," and the field was allowed to grow without interference. In the fall of 1979, it was mowed and baled before it went to seed. Shasta daisies were the sole survivors of the wild flowers and continue to appear.

RICHARD HAAG

Richard Haag, Prentice Bloedel, and Richard Brown consult on the north bluff road, 1980

At the same time as the bluff was being treated, the north drive road was re-aligned so that the meadow lying north of the guesthouse and the meadow north of the old road merged to form a much larger space. The road was graded in such a way that from the guesthouse, one could not see the road surface. The residue from the excavation was transported to build mounds that further screened the roadway north and east of the guesthouse. Haag was responsible for regrading and planting of these new mounds and directed extensive new tree planting in the meadow to the north along the new drive.

A new bridge was needed along this new north road. It was designed with heavy timbers in the oriental style. Mr. Bloedel was dissatisfied with its orientation — the alignment of the bridge with the center line of the new road did not please him, since the bridge was straight and the road was curved at that point. Soon after the bridge was completed, he even proposed removing it. Nevertheless, it remains to this day. Road alignment improvements have helped to mitigate the problem somewhat.

After the success of moving the north road, it was decided to tackle the entry drive, which Haag began to refer to as the "ceremonial walk." The expectation was that it could be driven on by dignitaries and invited guests — hence the name. Staff and other users of the house would approach it from the north or exit road, which had been designed with turnouts for vehicles to pass each other. Mrs. Bloedel thought the term "ceremonial walk" pompous and pretentious for what should have been a subtle, unobtrusive design element.

Haag proposed lowering the road south and west of the middle pond to the house in order to have it less noticeable, hidden from view from both the guesthouse and the main residence. At the entrance gates, the drive was narrowed to a minimum width of 12 feet. As it approached the guesthouse area, it widened to 14 feet. As the view of the middle pond emerged from trees, the road changed to 16 feet, enlarging finally to 20 feet as it

RICHARD HAAG

Regrading the east bluff

passed the parrot tree south of the middle pond. In addition, the road was lowered approximately 10 inches to nearly two feet. A crew removed eight hundred cubic yards of black crushed gravel that had built up from years of continuous road maintenance. The tucking of this road into the landscape represents a major contribution by Haag that cannot be fully appreciated without some knowledge of the previous condition of the road.

In 1981, a new "curved bridge" was constructed on the south drive below the guesthouse, designed to look as though there was no visible supporting structure. Isaacson Steel was engaged to engineer, design, construct, and install the bridge. It was preassembled and lifted onto footings at the site. Glue-laminated curved rails were formed to the precise radius of curvature of the road.

The east bluff as it appears today

Worker drills holes in the concrete channel to accommodate new moss.

The mossy area between the guesthouse and this bridge was at that time a plateau that featured a fiberglass-formed stream bed carrying the outlet waters of the Reflection Pool to the inlet of the Japanese Pool. To improve its appearance, the Reserve crew fabricated a new concrete stream channel. Mr. Bloedel later complained about the color of the concrete and the highly visible banks of the streambed. To solve these problems, holes were drilled into the concrete and were planted with Irish moss that had been previously used on the ground surrounding the stream. The planting provided a temporary moss groundcover until true mosses established themselves over time.

In December 1981, Mr. Bloedel designed a wooden bridge for the Christmas Pool, located at the bottom of the Rhododendron Glen. This plank bridge was to replace

The Christmas Pool bridge, 1985

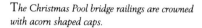

The Christmas Pool bridge railings are crowned with acorn shaped caps.

RICHARD BROWN

The Christmas Pool Bridge under construction.

RICHARD BROWN

an older arched bridge that was built too high above the water and too narrow for public use. The surface of the new bridge consisted of rough Douglas fir planks joined together lengthwise with oak keys. Mr. Bloedel wanted an oriental-style railing, and so, after many hours of consideration, he provided a simple sketch to Roats Engineering who, in turn, prepared construction drawings. Mr. Kaz Ishimitzu constructed the railings for the bridge from select, vertical grain clear redwood members.

In the spring of 1981, Haag's energies were directed toward improvements to the irrigation pond located at the southern end of the property. This pond was built in 1954 with assistance from the U.S. Soil Conservation Service for the purpose of providing irrigation water to the farm areas and to the nursery field located northwest of the main entrance. In view of the anticipated plantings that would occur as the Reserve prepared for public use, irrigation needs were projected to be greater over the next ten years or so than at any other time.

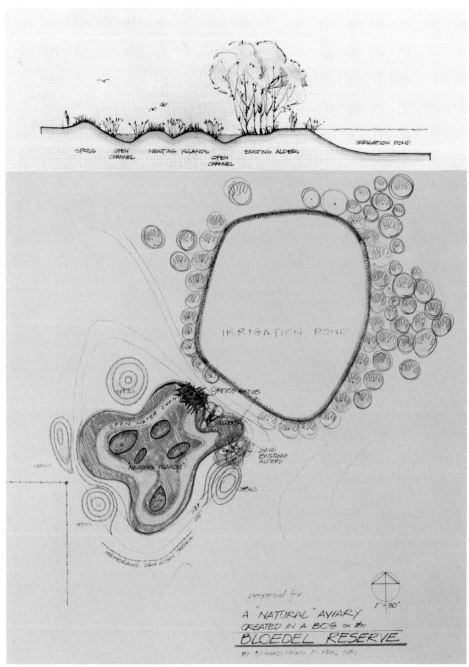

SPOILS · OPEN CHANNEL · NESTING ISLANDS · OPEN CHANNEL · EXISTING ALDERS · IRRIGATION POND

IRRIGATION POND

A "NATURAL" AVIARY
CREATED IN A BOG ON the
BLOEDEL RESERVE

*Richard Haag's proposal for a "natural"
aviary created in a bog on the Bloedel Reserve*

In considering the varied ways the old pond could be improved, the decision was made to create a water feature to attract and to provide appropriate habitat for birds, particularly water fowl. Haag's master plan proposal, prepared for his interview session with the Planning and Development Committee, had called for a "natural aviary" in this location. With recognition of the vegetation and habitats that were removed when the central parts of the Reserve were created, this proposed feature would be built for the birds first, and for man second. Haag recalls,

> As many times as I'd been coming out here, I never saw a red-winged blackbird. And that's a great symbol of spring. You've made it through another winter, and here comes this bird, all gaudy and squawking and screaming. So I told (Mr. Bloedel) we needed some blackbirds here and the first spring after completion they came in."

Unlike other projects assigned to Haag, development of this project proceeded without the extensive surveying and mapping that had preceeded work in other areas. Instead, Haag was able to "carve out" his design as he saw fit. Basic parameters were established that would include creation of islands for water fowl to nest on, excavation to depths necessary to reach water bearing sands, and excavation of small channels or "fingers of water" that would extend back into the alder tree line along the western shore of the proposed pond. Mr. Bloedel was intrigued by visions of water reaching back into the trees — a bayou type concept. Once the basic plan was approved, Dr. Frank Richardson — an ornithologist from the University of Washington — was invited to the Reserve to evaluate the site and these plans. He offered many useful suggestions pertaining to the planting plans and density of tree cover around the pool.

Excavation of the site progressed steadily until October, when heavy fall rains made the site impossible to work. The concept of fingers of waters never coalesced. The earth-moving machinery got stuck on the western side of the pool. Within a matter of a few days, rains filled the pond — nature's signal that it was "finished." The following spring, grading efforts removed the last evidence of use of heavy machinery and major plantings were installed. For the next three years, the site would rest and recover.

Prentice Bloedel and his granddaughter Lesley with Dr. Frank Richardson.

Dredging the Bird Sanctuary

The Bird Sanctuary islands as they appeared in 1983

A *tori gate and stone pathway provide a formal entry to the guesthouse and Japanese Gardens.*

The Garden of the Planes after completion

Also in 1981, Haag directed his energies to the creation of a garden on top of the old swimming pool to the north of the guesthouse. By the late 1970s, the pool system was old, with pipes breaking and leaks developing. The Bloedels contemplated whether to rebuild the pool or to replace it with something else. Haag suggested a Zen-style garden, replete with bamboo and an arrangement of stones. With no encouragement from Bloedel, Haag did not refine these initial concepts further.

Ink and wash sketch by Dr. Koichi Kawana of a proposed tori gate leading to the rock and sand Zen garden.

Dr. Kawana supervises placement of the stones in the Zen Garden.

Kawana plan view of dry garden of gravel and rocks, with granite edging, surrounded by existing mounds.

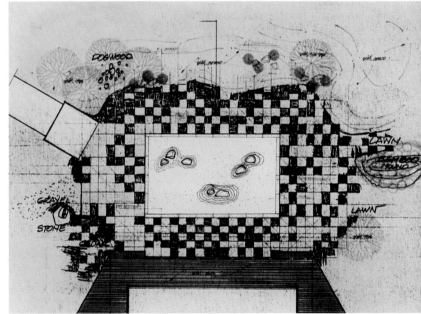

Instead, Haag derived an earth sculpture concept that he called the Garden of the Planes. He envisioned a garden with a random checkerboard pattern of alternating squares of moss and concrete surrounding a pyramidal mountain and valley. The design went through a number of changes before being executed in 1982. His original concept had been for two pyramids of equal size, one upright and the other inverted, both planted with moss. However, it was impossible to implement the plan within the existing rectangular space of the swimming pool. The staff could not reach consensus about what could be grown on the pyramids, considering the varied conditions that would affect growth. Consequently, the resulting earth sculpture was modified to be a truncated pyramid and inverted pyramid covered by crushed granite. Haag saw the pair as yin yang "held in a broken pattern of planes that call across to the blue fescue mound." From its inception, it had been a controversial resolution of the space, never having fully received the approval of the Board of Trustees. The planning committee, including Virginia Wright; Sally Schauman, a respected landscape architect and professor at the University of Washington; Mr. Bloedel; and Paul Kirk, had initially rejected the concept as being too artificial — it didn't seem to conform with anything else occurring in that part of the garden. Never officially approving of its design, the Board did allow a mock-up to be built in place for further review. This mock-up became the actual piece and remained on site for several years. One of the first changes effected by Environmental Planning and Design in 1986 was the hiring of Dr. Koichi Kawana, a professor of landscape architecture at the University of California at Los Angeles, to design and guide installation of the present rock and sand garden to replace Haag's Garden of Planes.

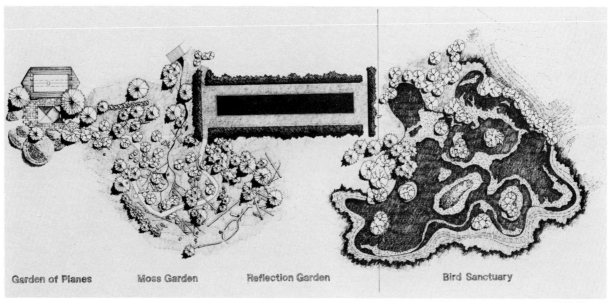

Garden of Planes   Moss Garden   Reflection Garden   Bird Sanctuary

A *series of gardens for the Bloedel Reserve by Richard Haag, 1985 submittal to American Society of Landscape Architects.*

The major work of 1982-83 was the Anteroom, now known as the Moss Garden. Haag and Brown had attended the Western Regional Meeting of the American Association of Botanical Gardens held at the University of British Columbia botanical garden in Vancouver, B.C. They were very impressed by the Nitobi Botanical Garden. In particular, they were struck by the quality of the moss; the roots and stems of huckleberry appeared almost black against this magnificent, velvet green moss floor. On their return, they discussed with Mr. Bloedel the idea of developing the moss garden to be a place where the native deciduous huckleberries, which were common on all the logs and stumps in the place, could be set off against a floor of moss. When Virginia and Bagley Wright returned from a trip to Japan, they shared pictures of Japanese moss gardens with Prentice Bloedel and discussed the possibilities. The concept was approved.

According to Richard Haag, the Anteroom was "created by selective subtractions of the nuances of nature from the chaos of a tangled bog." The work crew removed the indigenous salmonberry and underplanted the entire area with 275,000 starts of Irish moss, expecting true moss to invade it within five years, as it had along the guesthouse stream course. Some selective tree thinning was done of the alders, but a number were left cut off at

about 15 feet high to attract cavity nesting birds and woodpeckers. Hemlock, Douglas fir, and red cedar were planted in areas heavy with alders so that there would be, as Richard Brown put it, "a choreography, a dance of trees across the mossy space where large groupings of one species would dwindle in a direction to another species."

Prentice Bloedel took great interest in the project; he was very specific about the tree plantings in the space. He insisted on keeping the tall alder stumps over practically everybody's objection because he loved alders and thought their remains would provide an interesting, unusual environment. Mr. Bloedel suggested planting an understory tree. The alders and conifers would remain as the main overstory cover but, underneath that, other trees would be planted to provide shade for the future moss and filtered light for the huckleberries. At Mr. Bloedel's request, large-leaved Hercules walking stick trees were planted. They were expected in time to grow to 20 feet and convey an oriental character. Bloedel surprisingly insisted on a high density of planting — 100-200 trees in that acre. They located a source of four-foot high trees in New Orleans, and ordered 100. Locally, they found another dozen. The resulting canopy of trees above a rich green carpet of moss and ferns and decaying alder creates an extraordinary landscape.

MARY RANDLETT

RICHARD HAAG

A workman prepares the mosses for transplanting.

Newly planted mosses in the Anteroom

RICHARD HAAG

MARY RANDLETT

RICHARD BROWN

In 1986, Richard Haag was honored with the President's Award of Excellence from the American Society of Landscape Architects for the series of gardens he had worked on at the Reserve—the Garden of Planes, Anteroom, Reflection Garden, and Bird Sanctuary. Of these, only the Garden of the Planes was entirely his work and, as noted above, it had been replaced by the time of the awards. The original direction of pedestrian circulation through these spaces revealed a contrasting sequence of events beginning with the most abstract — the strong symbolism of the granite pyramids of the Plane Garden—and leading through the rich, lush decay and new growth of the Anteroom, then opening onto the formal geometry of the Reflection Garden and finally arriving at the natural environment of the Bird Sanctuary. Haag described the sequence,

> The gardens are extracted principles from our rich heritage of landscape form — providing living proof that man can be the steward of the land and can design with nature. To arouse latent emotional and aesthetic instincts and feelings, and to reaffirm man's immutable and timeless bond with nature, is implicit in its primary purpose.

The design jury was particularly impressed by

> … the one quality you see very, very rarely … the quality of soul or magical response. This project is made of that … It is where emotion and intelligence merge, which is probably what art's about … He has kept a very beautiful thought going. There is nothing

which is in or out of vogue. It is just a simple understanding of nature, of proportions, of art and of getting the most out of everything. This has great ecological logic. He didn't separate a knowledge of the ecological from knowledge of art. The work was heroic.

The last area to be developed on the property has been the Depression, a heavily forested section of ravine between the marsh and the bluff. Richard Brown recalls,

> We continued to discuss the other areas of the Reserve and walk them frequently, Haag, Mr. Bloedel and myself when possible. and when Haag wasn't around, Mr. Bloedel and I would walk through these areas, oftentimes for hours. We'd frequently start at 9:30 or 10:00 in the morning from the house, I with a machete, Mr. Bloedel with his walking stick, and we'd head off toward the depression or woods and would not return until lunch time.

While a number of concepts were discussed, nothing came of them for some time. Bloedel wished to reveal its natural beauty and looked at various trail courses to connect the bird marsh on the west to the waterfront bluff on the east. One of Mr. Bloedel's suggested trails followed the contour lines of the hilly site, but, on further investigation, this was found to be too "manipulative" a plan. One of the current changes proposed to the Reserve is the staking out of a trail and the building of a bridge over the ravine to finally open this area to the public.

CHAPTER 5

PLANNING FOR THE PUBLIC

In 1984, after a bout of illness, Mr. Bloedel decided to shed some of his business-related responsibilities and asked the Arbor Fund to find a replacement for him as President of the Board. Bagley Wright was eventually asked to replace him.

In the spring of 1985, a group of honorary advisors was invited to come and comment on the Reserve and its various projects—Arthur Erickson, Richard A. Howard, Russell J. Seibert, Mrs. Pendleton Miller, and Sir Peter Shepheard. The consensus was that the design solutions made in recent years were beginning to lose the sense of integrity that had been intended in the Reserve's purpose. They suggested the need for a master plan in the true sense of the word.

A committee of the Arbor Fund recommended the hiring of a private firm to prepare a master plan. As with the previous master plan process, proposals were solicited, this time from 16 local and national firms. Environmental Planning and Design of Pittsburgh was selected out of a group of six national and local finalists. The firm, established in 1939 by John and Philip Simonds, specializes in master planning and design for botanical gardens and arboreta, including the Chicago Botanical Garden, Missouri Botanical Garden, and Rancho Santa Ana Botanic Garden in California. Geoffrey Rausch, the partner in charge of the Bloedel design work, initially spent many hours walking the site with Mr. Bloedel. He learned that Mr. Bloedel was particularly concerned about certain areas that he felt were still in need of refinement, including the area between the Swan Pond and the exit road and the area that had been regraded at the east bluff. Mrs. Bloedel was concerned about the appearance of the Bird Marsh. Finally, large natural areas of the Reserve that were very special to Mr. Bloedel, including the Depression and the high points along Puget Sound, had still not been integrated into the trail system of the Reserve.

The intent of the Arbor Fund to open the property to the public meant that certain visitor facilities—parking, an interpretive center, and new access paths—were necessary. In the past, visitors would have proceeded down the drive to the house. From there, the Bloedels would have provided their guests with a guided walk through the property. While the main house was the obvious choice for a visitor center, the parking required to accommodate public access presented many aesthetic and functional problems. The solution was to create a gathering place remote from the house where cars could be parked and from which people would proceed on foot

Magnolia

78

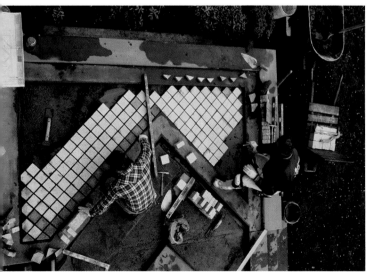

The vacant house awaits painters, carpenters, and floor refinishers in the fall of 1987.

Granite pavers are cut and installed to replace original concrete terraces surrounding the house.

to the house. Two sites were studied—the area adjacent to the main gate and the site of the maintenance barns at the end of the sheep meadow. Planning had actually progressed at the barn site to preliminary building plans when the Bloedels decided that the area at the gate should be reconsidered. The Bumgardner Architects was engaged to remodel the main house to receive visitors and accommodate the Reserve offices, as well as to design a new entrance building that would act as a gatehouse and orientation center.

According to Tim Hossner, the lead architect, the gatehouse was conceived as a pavilion in a park setting— its main room open, south-facing and sun-filled. While borrowing somewhat from the main residence its simple stuccoed exterior with cut masonry effects and segmental arched dormers, this building also fits easily into the more typical rural setting through the informal, asymetrical composition of its roofs and the exposed trusswork and beams of the interior. It provides an orientation point for visitors, who can examine a table-sized scale model of the property, pick up a map and guide, and learn through words and pictures about the history of the property and the intent of its owners. Along with the building of the gatehouse and orientation center, a new gate wall has been constructed that echoes the architecture of the house.

Framing complete, the gatehouse awaits its cement stucco facade.

RICHARD BROWN

TIM HOSSNER

Architect Tim Hossner's rendering shows the gatehouse, entrance wall and signage.

Pathways through the Forest

One of the most difficult problems facing the planners was the development of a main circulation route through the Reserve that would be relatively easy for the public to follow and also pass through the landscapes of the Reserve in a sequence that revealed Mr. Bloedel's desire that "... through study, understanding, and sympathetic treatment, the whole property would possess an internal unity and integrity that would realize its capacity to inspire and refresh." The main circulation route was conceived as an orchestration of landscape experiences weaving the natural areas into and out of the man-made gardens.

The sunlit field with the old barns at its end beckons the visitor from the gatehouse, the start of the main trail. The long walk down the field provides the opportunity for visitors to relax and unwind and to enter the world of the Bloedel Reserve. Large stands of quaking aspen in the large meadow to the northeast display delicately balanced large leaves that move in the lightest of breezes. There are many mature big leaf maples at the edge of the forest. Beyond the barns, the landscape begins to close in, the sunlight and openness are left behind, and the trail moves silently through a wilder section of forest; as it descends, the visitor catches first sight of the Bird Marsh.

MARY RANDLETT

The Bird Sanctuary in 1982, view to northwest

The Bird Sanctuary to the Swan Pond

Before the involvement of Environmental Planning and Design, the main approach to the Bird Marsh had been from the Reflection Pool down a service road through the woods. Visitors emerged onto a triangle of mowed grass at one end of the main pond and viewed across to the new islands in the distance. The islands and foreground were choked with cattails. From there, visitors retraced their steps and headed for the main house. The new trail winds down the hill between the firs to the west and emerges at the far end of the Bird Marsh. The first sight of the water is a long and dramatic vista between the alder islands to the open pond beyond. New planting has been added along the trail, including vine maples, native rhododendrons, and western red cedar. At the bottom of the slope, the path skirts the edge of the Bird Marsh. Once again the landscape is open and bright and full of the sound and movement of birds. The marsh has been redesigned to provide greater visual interest than before and to enable the visitor to see the birds at closer range. Large clumps of native vine maple have been planted on the left side of the path. The plantings, though still geared to attract birds, have been simplified and consolidated into masses. The cattails are confined to areas where they will not restrict views and have been removed from around the islands to reveal a simple composition of tall alder trunks softly fringed at the base with native sedges and ferns. The blackberries and salmonberry have been replaced with massings of the native blood currant, western azalea, and red osier dogwood grouped at the woods edge and hardhack spirea and moosewood viburnum at the water's edge.

The irrigation pond, 1982.

Resident family of geese on one of the several islands

A *red winged blackbird finds his perch on cattails.*

84

Alder stand at the Bird Sanctuary

The path continues around the Bird Marsh beneath a row of alder trees, then climbs into and passes through a dense forest typical of the Pacific Northwest region. Prentice Bloedel had envisioned this south wood area with a lake, but then had intuitively felt that such an element would change the character of the place too radically.

The Residential Landscape

Emerging from the forest, the visitor has a magnificent view of the main house in the distance across Middle Pond, the largest of the three lakes. On its far side are some handsome trees planted for their foliage and color. Particularly striking is the pendulous foliage of the weeping willow, which leafs out with soft greens in the early spring and becomes a rich golden yellow in the autumn. This tree provides a striking contrast at that season with the dark greens of the surrounding evergreens and the collection of copper and flame red colored Japanese maples at the head of the lower Swan Pond. At the edge of the drive and close to the pond are Dutch elm and parrot trees. On the right hand side of the drive is a pair of large Chinese magnolia.

The alignment of the drive creates a series of varied views, the house being visible across the lake. It is then lost from view as the drive curves around, concentrating attention on the trees on the lawn. Beyond, against the dark trees above the Swan Pond, are several purple leaf plums and a Chinese dogwood with its dense creamy-white flowers. One of the first areas Environmental Planning and Design addressed in its work at the Reserve was the Swan Pond edge. In 1985, the existing pebble beach at the east end was removed and the grade was changed slightly. To complement the landscape quality of the adjacent Middle Pond, several large boulders were carefully placed at the water's edge, and grass, accent shrubs and groundcover provide a simple and effective shore edge.

MARY RANDLETT

MARY RANDLETT

MARY RANDLETT

The golden leaves of the Katsura tree

RICHARD BROWN

Reaching the main house, the visitor is confronted with a more formal European landscape than previously experienced along the trail. Flanking the main facade are Empress trees. On the lawn are two Dutch elms. Across the drive adjacent to a short stairway and retaining wall on the west side is a large 'Pink Diamond' rhododendron. This was one of the most popular hybrids raised at Leonardslee in Sussex by Sir Edmund Loder. In front of this mass of shrubs is a young Katsura tree, a very handsome ornamental that can attain a height of 100 feet. Its leaves turn a brilliant golden in autumn. Also to the west of the house, opposite the Dutch elms, is a very large Portuguese laurel.

Flanking the north terrace of the house are two

The east terrace, 1981

View of the east bluff as it is today

*Cherry tree and espalier apple tree at south
end of the house*

Camperdown elms with domed, worked heads on a straight elm stock, a hybrid form that was popular in England from the early nineteenth century. Below the lookout terrace the steep slopes are planted thickly with St. John's wort. At the foot of the slope, what was an orchard in the time of Mrs. Collins has been re-graded to create an undulating grassy meadow, flanked on either side by large mounds. The forms of the meadow and the mounds were designed to lead the eye toward the two 'windows' of the Sound. These window-like views are framed by the native woods at the top of the bluff and by a clump of fir trees. Beyond the hedge are specimen Stranvaesia trees and an early flowering cherry. Against the garage wing area are a series of flowering cherries and camellias.

Birch trees embellish the path along the east bluff.

Into the Depression and onto the Bluff

A path beside the garage leads into the forest south of the house. This was Mr. Bloedel's "walk in the woods." When Environmental Planning and Design began work at the Reserve, Mr. Bloedel was concerned that the experience of the Reserve would not be complete without making the "wild areas" accessible, so that the visitor could experience the undulating topography and the hemlocks, vine maples, and alders that grew naturally in it. A loop trail had been considered for some time, a major obstacle being a thirty-foot-deep ravine spanning a small creek. Many routes through this depression had been staked over the years. Ken Caldwell, a local landscape architect, had catalogued every feature and developed a rating scale for describing uniqueness. Every stump, tatoosh, fallen log, and major tree was mapped and annotated. With that knowledge, Environmental Planning and Design staked out a woodland trail system that now winds through the mature forest past massive stumps and trunks, leads down a sheer maple slope and across alder wetlands, climbs to the tops of Fir Hill and

Fern Hill with their views across Puget Sound, skirts the edge of a sedge bog, and finally emerges on the east bluff behind the main house.

The grassy meadow between the bluff walk and the hill is the result of regrading under Richard Haag's direction. It is graced at its edge with Sadler oaks, Hinoki cypress trees, and, at its north edge, a grove of Himalayan birch trees with their striking white, peeling bark. These were removed from the Bird Marsh and transplanted here to reinforce the axis from the house to the water defined by the mounding of field grasses and the curvilinear "river" of mowed turf. Mr. Bloedel had been trying to develop a second axis running north/south along the meadow. Environmental Planning and Design has planted the site of the former tennis courts to bring it into balance with the sedge bog to the south that opens a finger into the forest. Rhododendron Glen has been cut off from the field above by the planting of a grove of Japanese maples given by Mrs. Bloedel. Guarding entry to the Glen are large leaved, white flowering hydrangeas and shadbushes, trees with abundant and showy flowers in early spring.

DICK BUSHER

The north terrace steps are inlaid with moss
and framed by saxifrage.

Azaleas and Oxalis in the Glen

MARY RANDLETT

Waterfall in the Glen

Ferns are nurtured in their growth by an old
maple tree in Rhododendron Glen.

Rhododendron Glen and Orchid Walk

Environmental Planning and Design did little to change the old sequence of trails prepared by the Bloedels that carry the visitor from the main house through the Glen, up Mr. Church's trail through the Douglas firs, and into the Japanese Garden.

From the lawn fronting the north terrace of the house, the visitor descends a flight of stairs flanked by American chestnut trees. The banks are covered with a thick mat of lily-turf, a grass-like perennial that grows in mats and provides a striking textural contrast to the very dark, upright dwarf forms of the Hinoki cypress that march down the slope toward the Sound.

The path leads to the Glen, where the bulk of the rhododendron collection is planted beneath trees of second-growth timber. Surrounded by a thick planting of rhododendrons and maples — many of which were Mrs. Collins' prized specimens nearer the house — the man-made waterfall below the drive seems native to the place, although it was built in 1954 as part of the damming project. Its waters are the overflow for the chain of lakes above.

The path to the right leads into and through the forest and emerges on the bluff below the hill on which the house sits, passing the site of the former tennis courts where Mrs. Collins first thought about building her house.

MARY RANDLETT

Wildflowers blanket the former site of the tennis court.

MARY RANDLETT

94

Christmas Pool in late spring

The Rhododendron Glen is an area of logged-over forest, from which several stumps remain and beneath which many hybrid and species rhododendrons have been planted. The conditions here in the half light of the forest are very similar to the natural habitat of many rhododendrons, although the rainfall here is lighter. As the path dips toward a small stream, the visitor approaches a bench set below a bank of yellow cowslip primroses.

One of the garden's attractive built features is a bridge over the Christmas Pool. The pool was a Christmas present from Mr. Bloedel to his wife in 1970. The bridge overlooks one of the two principal creeks in the Glen — creeks planted lavishly with water-loving plants. Up the trail from the Christmas Pool, the visitor sees a variety of common and rare rhododendrons that provide splendid color displays in April and May. One of the most spectacular plants, Rhododendron calophytum, grows up to 40-feet-high, with leaves one foot long and broad bell-shaped white to rose flowers. Its first flowering in England in the early years of this century excited a number of the leading rhododendron fanciers, Lionel Rothschild, Gerald Loder, I. Godman, and Ludwig Messel. They were invited by Loder to a house party at Wakehurst Place in Sussex, where they walked solemnly around the splendid plant raising their hats to it!

In addition to the permanent display of rhododendrons, this area has the largest display of hardy cyclamen in the Pacific Northwest, several species of trillium, lung worts, azaleas, red vein enkianthus, and a splendid display of native wild ginger.

Standing at the exit of the Rhododendron Glen is a magnificent clump of large Japanese maples, beautifully pruned to form open umbrella-like structures supporting their foliage. Nearby and along the drive are examples of the largest and most tropical-looking of the magnolias — the Big Leaf magnolia.

*Candelabra primulas and rhododendrons
enliven the verdant environs of the Glen.*

Mrs. Bloedel's viewing room to the Swan Pond

The orchids that give Orchid Walk its name

Stepping stones lead from Orchid Walk into the Zen Garden.

Orchid Walk, originally known as Church Walk, leads from the Rhododendron Glen to the guesthouse. The path moves through a second-growth forest that has been cleaned out and underplanted with a few rhododendrons. Shortly after leaving the drive, the visitor finds a very small and intimate space to the left that provides a good view of the Swan Pond. Environmental Planning and Design created this sitting area as Mr. Bloedel's birthday gift to his wife. Mrs. Bloedel had particularly liked sitting under the shade of the old hemlock and contemplating the view across the pond. Here, the designers have placed a small wood bench. Tucked in around the bench clearing are some of Mrs. Bloedel's favorite plants — skimmia, native azaleas, hardy cyclamen, and trillium.

Further on, a short flight of steps leads to a glade stretching down to the lakes. It is planted on both sides with maples and is especially colorful in the autumn. Beyond this glade, the path leads to a plantation of tall firs closely planted together. The low light level of the foliage of these trees has prevented any growth on the forest floor. It is covered with needles, and the path is virtually indistinguishable from the ground to either side. Native coralroot orchids have established here. It is a simple but very powerful landscape. The path emerges from the forest past stands of bamboo and conifers to the light and openness of the large meadow beyond, defined by stands of quaking aspen trees.

98

Dr. Kawana's rock and sand Zen garden

Visitors stroll along the path at the Japanese Gardens.

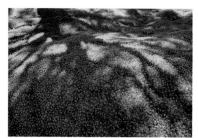

MARY RANDLETT

MARY RANDLETT

The Japanese Gardens

The stone and sand garden and its surroundings fronting the guesthouse evoke the meditative quality of such Eastern gardens. The western edge of the space is defined by low mounds planted with dwarf rockspray cotoneaster and bolax, an alpine from the Falkland Islands. Beyond is a very large mound, also covered with the cotoneaster, but originally planted with blue sheep fescue in an attempt to relate this mound to the pair of large blue Atlas Cedar trees beside the guest house deck. The southern boundary of this space is defined by a low wooden fence bound together with thongs in the traditional Japanese fashion.

From the east side of the guesthouse deck, the visitor can view the main part of the Japanese garden designed by Kubota. In traditional Japanese gardens, the visitor walks slowly so that each subtly framed view can be experienced. In theory there is an infinite number of different visual compositions that can occur, symbolically emphasizing the diversity and continuity of nature. The experience of walking around the edge of this pond is one in which the view continually changes, being articulated by subtle shifts in the alignment of the path and the mounds alongside it. The landscape is traditionally planted with pruned pine trees and shrubs and carefully placed rocks. Against the dark backdrop of coniferous trees, the Japanese maple provides bold color contrast, particularly in the autumn. The planting has been skillfully arranged so that the visitor cannot see either of the other lakes or the main house.

MARY RANDLETT

The ambiance of the Japanese Garden changes with the seasons.

MARY RANDLETT

Although the Japanese Garden had been approached from Orchid Walk for many years, that route did not provide a formal sense of entry. At the suggestion of Environmental Planning and Design, Dr. Kawana has designed a new gate and fence and has reworked the path, installing stepping stones in the grass paths in anticipation of the increase in foot traffic that comes with the opening of the Reserve to the public. From the guesthouse, the visitor exits beneath a wooden arch, reminescent of a tori gate. A large Mugo pine, dogwood trees, and moss groundcover provide a sense of closure to the Oriental ambiance.

View to the Anteroom from the tori gate

MARY RANDLETT

MARY RANDLETT

RICHAR

Aralia *in the moss forest.*

Moss Garden and Reflection Pool

As the path moves through the Japanese Garden, across the main drive to the Moss Garden, and finally reaches the Reflection Pool, it leads the visitor through a sequence of experiences that becomes progressively more pared-down and introspective. In the shade and muffled sound of the Moss garden, large tree remains have been allowed to lie on the ground so that the natural processes of decay may continue. The combination of vine maple, Hercules walking stick, huckleberry, and the tall stumps of alder trees contributes a somewhat exotic character to the wood. This is enhanced by the native mosses on the forest floor. The Moss Garden path leads to the Reflection Pool and its surround of clipped yew hedges. Their presence defines the space, carving it out of the dense forest which rears up behind the hedge. This is one of the most memorable spaces in the Reserve and the appropriate, final manmade garden in the carefully orchestrated sequence of paths. On leaving the Reflection Pool, the visitor sees the delicate forms and color of paper birch contrasting with the darkness of the forest behind and passes by dark, glossy-leaved camellias. These ornamental plants are soon left behind, and the path continues on through a native alder grove, emerging into the full sun of the meadow where it began.

MARY RANDLETT

The Reflection Pool tames the forest with its geometric precision and the stillness of its ground waters.

EPILOGUE

A GIFT FOR THE FUTURE

The shaping of this extraordinary property into its present form owes much to the vision and persistence of Prentice and Virginia Bloedel. In particular, it has grown naturally and instinctively from their initial and continuing clarity about the goal they wished to achieve in all the work that was to go on at the Reserve over many decades.

> … to set the land aside for the primary purpose of providing others with the opportunity to enjoy plants both as arranged by man and as they arrange themselves; and for the purpose of providing people wandering about the Reserve a refreshing experience of nature and a broadening of their appreciation of their world.

In order for the vision to become reality, the Bloedels relied upon the forces of a great many talented and skilled architects, landscape architects, botanists, designers, nursery and craftspeople, grounds maintenance crews, and dedicated board members. Each of these people has had an impact upon the Reserve; the qualities of its spaces are best described as having been shaped by teams working together. It is clear too that for all that is visible on the Reserve property, there is also what we might call "the unbuilt Reserve," many projects that were proposed and rejected in the Bloedel's search for the proper forms — ones that would be eloquent, subtle, and appropriately humble embellishments — landscapes that would honor and respect the wildness of the native forest which is at the heart of the Reserve.

For the public who come here, it is important to recognize the great amount of committed time, energy, and devotion that has gone into safeguarding this land from development in perpetuity. The carefully considered planning that led to the establishment of the Arbor Fund and the guidelines by which it acts will allow for the continued maintenance of the property as its owners wish. It will guarantee that future generations will have

the same pleasure you experience today of seasonal color, varied spaces, glades, ponds, and vistas. It will make the lovely house and grounds a congenial meeting place for symposia, instruction, and receptions. And if, as you walk in the hushed shelter of giant cedars and hemlocks or sit on the bank of Orchid Walk watching the swans in the pond below, you happen to sense some presence other than your own, it may be the "poet or dreamer" breathing deeply as he or she reflects on the satisfaction that comes of having created from the wilderness a place perfectly suited to the appreciation of wild and gentle nature.

Oxalis

A garden that one makes oneself becomes associated with one's personal history, and that of one's friends interwoven with one's tastes, preferences, and character, and constitutes a sort of unwritten but withal manifest autobiography. Show me your garden, provided it be your own, and I will tell you what you are like.

Alfred Austin

APPENDIX

FEATURED PLANTS AT THE BLOEDEL RESERVE

The Glen   Rhododendron, Cyclamen, Trillium, lungworts, Pieris, Enkianthus, ferns, and Primula

Japanese Garden   Pinus, Bolax, Cotoneaster, Arctostaphylos, Fragaria, mosses, wintergreen, Katsura tree

Moss Garden   Mosses, ferns, conifers, deciduous trees, Aralia

Bird Marsh   Amelanchier, Typha, Iris, Cornus, Rhododendron occidentale, Mahonia, Salal, Indian Plum, aquatic perennials

Reflection Garden   Taxus hedge, Trillium, Anemone, Oxalis, Camellia, violets, bluebells

Residence Garden   Elms, cherries, boxwood, Primula, beech, Liriope, Paulownia, Hinoki cypresses, Lithodora, Portuguese laurel, Rhododendron, Magnolia

SOURCES

Bloedel, Prentice. "The Bloedel Reserve – Its Purpose Its Future," *U.W. Arboretum Bulletin*, Spring, 1980.

Bloedel, Prentice. "Some Aspects of Conservation," an address to the University of Washington Forest Club and College of Forestry Alumni Association, March 5, 1955.

Frey, Susan Rademacher. "A Series of Gardens," *Landscape Architecture*, (Washington, D.C.: American Society of Landscape Architects), September/October 1986.

Holmes, J. Lister. *The Tale of an Estate*, unpublished essay, Sept. 1977, Bloedel Reserves Archives.

Journal of John Work, a Chief Trader of the Hudson's Bay Company during his expedition from Vancouver to the Flatheads and Blackfeet of the Pacific Northwest, ed. by William S. Lewis and Paul C. Phillips. Cleveland (Arthur Clark Co.), 1923.

Lockman, Heather. "Gardens: Nature in Gentle Custody: Shaping the Bloedel Reserve in Puget Sound," *Architectural Digest*, June, 1984.

MacKay, Donald. *Empire of Wood: The MacMillan Bloedel Story*. (Seattle: University of Washington Press) 1982.

Willis, Elizabeth Bayley and Pam Price. "A Brief Report on the Early History of the Bloedel Reserve Deeds," research files and documents, Bloedel Reserve Archives.

J. Lister Holmes papers, Archives and Manuscripts Collection, University of Washington.

J. Lister Holmes architectural drawings, Special Collections, University of Washington.

Washington State Biography files, Special and Northwest Collections, University of Washington (John Collins, Mrs. John Collins, Bertrand Collins, Julius Bloedel, Prentice Bloedel).

Transcripts of interviews conducted by Mary Randlett with Virginia Clarke Younger in 1977 and 1987. Bloedel Reserve Archives.

Landscape plans, drawings, and renderings, Bloedel Reserve Archives.

Ito, Kazuo. *Issei, History of Japanese Immigrants in North America*. Seattle: Japanese Community Service, *1973*.

ILLUSTRATION AND PHOTOGRAPHY CREDITS

The following people and organizations have provided original photography, artwork, and/or illustration materials.

Bloedel Reserve Archives

Richard Brown

Photography by Dick Busher. Courtesy of ARCHITECTURAL DIGEST. © 1984. All rights reserved. Architectural Digest Publishing Corporation.

Casper Clarke

Greg Gilbert

Richard Haag

Tim Hossner

Robert Peckham

Mary Randlett

Suquamish Tribal Photographic Archives

Virginia Wright

Asahel Curtis Collection, Washington State Historical Society

Botanical Prints courtesy
Special Collections and Preservation Division,
University of Washington Libraries:

> *Flora Londinensis containing A History of the Plants indigenous to Great Britain*, Wm. Curtis, F.L.S., George Graves, editor. London, 1817, vol. 1.

> *The Botanical Magazine or Flower Garden Displayed.* William Curtis, F.L.S., (later Samuel Curtis), various volumes, London 1787-1827.

Edward Curtis Neg. No. NA 321
Port Madison Neg. No. 8882
T. Prosch Neg. No. NA 1366

THE ARBOR FUND

ABOUT THE AUTHOR AND THE PRINCIPAL PHOTOGRAPHER

Lawrence Kreisman is an architectural historian, historic preservation consultant, and teacher. He attended The City College of New York and holds a Masters Degree in Literature from the University of Chicago and a Masters degree in Architecture from the University of Washington. His publications include *Historic Preservation in Seattle, West Queen Anne School: Renaissance of a Landmark, Art Deco Seattle,* and *Apartments by Anhalt.* He is currently co-authoring *Architecture and Children,* a curriculum guide for teachers. Mr. Kreisman is a lecturer in the Department of Urban Design and Planning at the University of Washington and conducts history and architectural tours throughout the Northwest. Through his publications, courses, and tours, he has encouraged people to be aware of the richness and diversity of historically and architecturally important resources and to value their preservation.

Mary Randlett was the 1983 recipient of the Governor's Award for her "unique contribution to the field of photography." Her subjects include nature, architecture, children and families, and a unique documentary of the region's creative people — poets, artists, writers, and architects photographed in their studios or working environments. Her photographs are held in more than 30 permanent collections nation-wide, including the Metropolitan Museum of Art, the Smithsonian Institution, and major Pacific Northwest collections. Ms. Randlett's work has been widely published in books, magazines, and newspapers. These include *The House Next Door, Downtown Seattle Walking Tours, Historic Preservation in Seattle,* and the forthcoming *Art in Seattle's Public Places.*